TANTRA EXPOSED

TANTRA EXPOSED

The Enlightening Path of Tantra
Unveiling the Practical Guide to Eternal Bliss

- SERENADE OF BLISS BOOK 4 -

SANTATAGAMANA

Editor: Eric Robins

Disclaimer for Legal Purposes

The information provided in this book is strictly for reference only and is not in any manner a substitute for medical advice. In the case of any doubt, please contact your healthcare provider. The author assumes no responsibility or liability for any injuries, negative consequences or losses that may result from practicing what is described in this book. Any perceived slights of specific people or organizations are unintentional. All the names referred to in this book are for illustrative purposes only, are the property of their respective owners and not affiliated with this publication in any way.

Read also, by the same author of this book:

REAL YOGA SERIES

— KRIYA YOGA EXPOSED
The Truth about current Kriya Yoga Gurus & Organizations. Contains the explanation of Kriya Yoga techniques, including the Final Special Kriya.

— THE SECRET POWER OF KRIYA YOGA
Revealing the Fastest Path to Enlightenment. How Fusing Bhakti & Jnana Yoga into Kriya will Unleash the most Powerful Yoga Ever.

— KUNDALINI EXPOSED
Disclosing the Cosmic Mystery of Kundalini. The Ultimate Guide to Kundalini Yoga & Kundalini Awakening.

— THE YOGA OF CONSCIOUSNESS
25 Direct Practices to Enlightenment. The ultimate guide to Non-Duality (Advaita).

— TURIYA: THE GOD STATE
Unravel the ancient mystery of Turiya - The God State. The book that demystifies and uncovers the true state of Enlightened beings.

SERENADE OF BLISS SERIES

— SAMADHI: THE FORGOTTEN EDEN
Revealing the Ancient Yogic Art of Samadhi.

— THE YOGIC DHARMA: THE SUPREME YAMAS AND NIYAMAS
A profound, unconventional, & inspiring exposition on the Yogic Dharma principles.

— LUCID DREAMING: THE PATH OF NON-DUAL DREAM YOGA
Lucid dreaming like you've never seen before. The complete alchemical elixir: Transform Lucid Dreaming into Non-dual Dream Yoga.

All of these books are available @ Amazon as Kindle & Paperback.

Subscribe and receive the eBook **Uncovering the Real** plus updates and information regarding new books or articles, which will be sent about once a month.

www.RealYoga.info

If you have any doubts or questions regarding this or any of the other books, feel free to contact me at:

Santata@RealYoga.info

Special thanks to Eric Robins, who edited and proofread this book with profound love, kindness, and dedication. Your help has been invaluable.

Tell me what you know,
and then I will teach you what is beyond that.

- CHANDOGYA UPANISHAD

TABLE OF CONTENTS

INTRODUCTION

Near the top of a very tall tree somewhere in North America, there was a large nest built by a red-tailed hawk. It was early April and the last egg of three had just been laid. Unfortunately, due to raging storm winds, the egg was blown out of the nest and into the yard of a nearby farm. Seeing the egg, one chicken decided to incubate it. In time, the egg finally hatched, and the baby hawk was raised by chickens, believing itself to be one of them.

Although the hawk loved to watch other birds flying above, it never imagined that it could fly. One day, years later, a flying hawk was passing by and saw our confined, farm-raised hawk. Without any hesitation, the flying hawk decided to land on the farm and show the farm-raised hawk who it really was and where it truly belonged: soaring free in the sky.

The vast majority of human beings are like that farm-raised hawk: although they are capable of flying freely in the sky, they live confined on the ground. But there's a way to change that. That way is called Tantra.

You've probably already heard of or read about Tantra. It is a powerful buzzword. But like most buzzwords, it has been misrepresented and bathed in sensationalism.

Nowadays, there are two main forms of "Tantra" that are shared all over the world:

1. The westernized, sexualized, modern branch found on the Internet and in books, which is what most people think about when they hear the word "Tantra."

2. The scholarly, rigid, more complex branch typically found in large, dense books, often written by translators or pundits, and where classic tantric texts are interpreted and expounded upon.

There's nothing wrong with either of these two types of Tantra; each has its place depending on what you're looking for. However, it's hardly surprising that the first form of Tantra does not depict a proper or effective path toward Self-Realization. And it's no wonder that spiritual tomes often end up unfinished and accumulating dust on the shelf. Sometimes, they have the misfortune of causing unintended effects: they enmesh you even more deeply into the Mayic web through their complex and often draining verbiage.

This volume, however, belongs to a third category. It is an easily digestible book that brings to light a practical path toward awakening from the slumber of ignorance. It will show you how to overcome suffering, transcend your current limits, and experience the ecstatic bliss and wholeness inherent in your true nature.

The Tantra presented in this book does not necessarily attempt to strictly reproduce the old methodologies of tantric traditions, which are often needlessly mystified. Rather, its goal is to equip you with teachings and practices that are better suited to today's culture, understanding, and actual practical use.

I'm not interested in giving you a history lesson on Tantra or its sects; I'm not interested in giving a sermon on why Tantra is ethically good or bad; and I'm not interested in perpetuating misinformation concerning Tantra. I am only interested in sharing my experience and insight into Tantra as a way to guide you toward the realization of who you really are. The wisdom presented in this book doesn't come from secondhand knowledge, but rather is drawn from my own journey, direct experience, and inner knowing. I want to leave Tantra wide open, visible, uncovered—exposed.

This book is for those who are thirsty to embark on a real spiritual journey and unravel the mystery of Tantra.

There comes a moment in your life when your desire for completeness expands past conventional seeking; when you feel a calling to explore beyond the known and visible; when you decide that it's time to leave the farm and explore the sky. If you are reading this book, then chances are that such a yearning has already been awakened. If so, then this is your book—it is the *liberating* flying hawk.

Let's unfold Tantra together.

Part 1

Discovering the Real Tantra

Like oil in sesame seeds, butter in cream, water in the river bed, fire in tinder, the Self dwells within the soul.

- SHVETASHVATARA UPANISHAD

CHAPTER 1

PLENITUDE OF BEING

Everybody longs for happiness.

It doesn't matter what country you were born in, the color of your skin, or the genre you identify with; it doesn't matter the level of education you possess, the amount of money you have, or the kind of job you go to every day; it doesn't matter what you believe in, the type of thoughts that dwell in your mind, or how spiritually advanced you are—you are always looking for happiness. That's always the goal. You strive for what you believe will complete you.

The truth of the matter is that whenever we feel perfectly realized—we are perfectly happy. When we feel realized, life flows effortlessly, the aroma of bliss permeates through each of our actions, and our mind's waves are calm, peacefully hugging the shore of life. In these moments, we have no desire other than just being and enjoying this blissful *is-ness*.

Is realization a consequence of happiness, or is happiness caused by realization? Happiness and realization are synonymous; they are two words that represent the same state of completeness. You can't be fully realized without being happy, and you can't be fully happy without being realized.

There are many moments throughout our lives when we feel realized, regardless of whether this lasts for only a couple of minutes or for weeks at a time. This occurs particularly during three types of situations:

1. When we accomplish something that we truly wanted. I.e., when we fulfill our current desire. Oh, don't we experience total delight in such situations?

2. When we connect with someone we love. It can be as simple as looking deeply into their eyes, holding their hands, giving them a big hug, or through lovemaking. I.e., our sense of identity and preservation lies not only within us but also in someone else, and thus when we connect with them, we're reuniting our sense of self and feeling complete.

3. When something greater than us occurs, which puts us totally in the present moment. I.e., When we are in awe due to some amazing occurrence or event.

However, these experiences of realization are fleeting. They're but a moment, and like all moments, they soon fade into incompleteness. Sometimes, you may not even know exactly what you want or need, but you rationalize it into some specific desire that needs to be fulfilled. There's just this constant sense of uneasiness that tells us that we must "find that which gives us happiness and fulfillment." Attaining a level of realization through the conquest of desires, by connecting with someone we love, or due to some wonderful occurrence is really just a temporary painkiller. We may indeed experience happiness during those moments, but it ends way too soon.

Inevitably, we find ourselves again and again back in the search for fulfillment. It's as if every time we're about to fill our "container of contentment," it grows larger and can never really get filled. Can we ever fill this ever-growing container through such means? Can the continuous craving for something outside of ourselves somehow fulfill the ravenous void that every human experiences?

By following this "sense of lack" back to its source, we find the underlying reason for its existence: our original nature as unbounded consciousness apparently contracted and fragmented itself into our individual and limited form, and now, we are left with an inherent feeling and longing to expand and be whole again.

You may not be aware of it yet, but there will come a time

when these types of ephemeral blisses will no longer cut it for you. They function like a drug, always making you crave them more and more, always dependent on external factors to be achieved—which are truly out of your control.

To surpass this normal level of bliss, we need to step into a deeper form of realization: Self-Realization.

There are many paths toward Self-Realization, and one of the most powerful is the path of Tantra. Tantra covers a broad spectrum of spiritual teachings and practices, integrating with countless other genuine paths. If approached and used correctly, it unleashes the unlimited reservoir of bliss in us, allowing us to tap into this supreme realization of our Self— into perfect realization, perfect happiness, and perfect fulfillment. And what does *perfect* mean? It means that it doesn't end. Perfect realization is unending happiness.

You are reading this book because you've opened up to the spiritual dimension of your life, and you want to dive even deeper into it; you want to know what Tantra really is and how it can help blossom the flower of your existence. You have the innate desire to wake up to your true self, which itself is the very "experience" of Self-Realization, and to break free from the vacuum of incompleteness.

This longing to awaken to your original state of happiness

will guide you into your own being, allowing you to fall in love with it and with your inner dimension, and unfolding a never-ending dance of peaceful rapture. This is the type of longing that Tantra celebrates unconditionally, not only opening up a path to realize your undying Self, but also propelling you to be your purest expression within this dual world by truly embodying your realization. Let's discover the lyrics of this tantric song of the heavens.

"You do not acquire happiness.
Your very nature is happiness."

- RAMANA MAHARSHI,
TALKS WITH SRI RAMANA MAHARSHI

CHAPTER 2

THE PURPOSE OF TANTRA

The word *Tantra* has become synonymous with sex in western society. Go to any website, book, or class that mentions Tantra, and you'll most likely be presented with information on how to achieve a more powerful and lasting orgasm, how to use "ancient tantric teachings" to improve your sex life or intimate relationships, or how to have "spiritual sex." However, such presentations of Tantric teachings seldom bear any resemblance to the actual teachings that will lead a practitioner to Self-Realization.

The goal of Tantra is not to step up your sex life, nor is it at all related to seductiveness or sensual massages. Of course, many people experience a lot of sexual repression, so "Tantra" workshops that specialize in this may help to liberate those tensions[1]. However, that's not the original purpose of Tantra.

---

[1] Always tread these waters carefully, as there are plenty of charlatans.

In fact, the gap between what is typically taught versus the actual tantric teachings that can lead a seeker to Self-Realization is continually growing, leading to great misunderstanding.

Tantra has the purpose of deepening your connection with your own being; of unfolding a path toward realizing your true Self. It has nothing to do with sex in and of itself. The bliss experienced through the buildup of sexual energy achieved through sex can serve as a vehicle for a higher state of consciousness but so can many other means. It's no surprise that society has managed to look at Tantra, and what they seemingly boiled it down to was: sex. A similar phenomenon happened with Yoga, where only the first limb out of eight from Patanjali's Yoga Sutras is highlighted worldwide—asanas—and turned into a physical fitness discipline. It's as if humanity is conditioned to look at a rose, and instead of taking in its beauty, fragrance, and delicacy, we look at its thorns.

Tantra can be divided into various systems and explained in innumerable ways. Because of its vast scale, it's hard to confine Tantra to a particular school, procedure, methodology, or teaching. The guidance in this book goes in the direction of nondual Tantra since this is the highest type of tantric teachings when one's purpose is enlightenment.

The word "Tantra" can be used to mean "doctrine" or "book," but also "continuum." *Tan* (continuation, expansion), *Tra* (instrument of, save, protection). Tantra allows the seeker to expand their consciousness (= tan) into the broader universal field of consciousness and save themselves from ignorance/protect themselves from Maya (= tra); it is an instrument that provides us with a way to realize the unbroken continuation of consciousness. However, in the general sense, Tantra is a word that implies a specific set of spiritual practices and teachings, and depending on the time, setting, tradition, and the one teaching it, it can designate different methodologies toward enlightenment.

Fundamentally, Tantra is a type of spiritual teaching that instructs us how to become aware of *plenitude* (i.e., how to tap into the blissful and fulfilling state of "realization") and then expand it until it swallows our "I-ness," leaving a transcendental, transpersonal, selfless bliss-consciousness in its place. Tantra seeks to illuminate our mind in order to allow it to *touch* its source of ecstatic emptiness, melting its gross layers of ego-based conditioning, and opening our wings of freedom toward Self-Realization. It is a vehicle of transcendence, but also of actualization of our dualistic potential in this lifetime—it eternally dances in form and formlessness. It is living nonduality within duality without having to dissolve the experience of the latter.

25

Have you ever wondered, "Who am I?", "Why am I here?", "How can I achieve everlasting happiness?", "How can I eradicate suffering from my life once and for all?", or "How can I truly be what I know I am?" Intellectual or written answers will never satisfy you. But Tantra has the keys to answer those questions; it provides you with a way to experience the source of your being and gives you the wisdom and the understanding of the existence of dual experience.

Tantra practitioners don't need to abolish duality or the world from their lives; they don't need to keep themselves from expressing gratitude for and enjoying all the facets of their existence. Many spiritual disciplines make you turn your back on the world and tell you that you should not enjoy the world or your dualistic existence (e.g., by practicing asceticism). This is not the case with Tantra.

Tantra expands and illuminates our relationship with the world. It allows us to experience and engage with the world without a limiting and self-centered filter. Even for those who have an awakened discernment and know their true nature, the flow of cosmic wisdom and awe will never stop arriving from within.

This is real Tantra.

CHAPTER 3

TANTRIC INITIATION, SHAKTIPAT, AND GURU

"In the monastery of your heart, you have a temple
where all Buddhas unite."

- MILAREPA,
THE LIFE OF MILAREPA

All human beings have the potential to be enlightened. Although it's a remarkably rare occurrence, so is life itself. Enlightenment, or Self-Realization, signifies discontinuation from the current dense evolutive progression into a completely distinct state of being.

The first time this discontinuation occurs is during *shaktipat* ("Descent of Energy/Grace"), which is often thought to occur during tantric initiation.

Some seekers think that tantric initiation is when a consort (customarily a woman) initiates the seeker (typically a man) into Tantra through a sexual act. Although there may be some form of "Tantra" out there employing such methods, this far from the actual nondual Tantra taught in this book.

The actual tantric initiation, just like in many yogic traditions, may also be thought of as a religious or mystic ritual wherein the Guru initiates the disciple into a practice and teaching, sometimes awakening the student's latent life-force, chakras, or third-eye in the process, by giving shaktipat. Oftentimes, this is preceded by a purification rite and the taking of sacred vows.

Although initiation is traditionally understood as an intimate and in-person guru-to-disciple transmission (which is normally true and often required), this is but a symbolic representation of the deeper transmission that occurs. The communication that transpires between an enlightened being and a disciple is one of communion, beyond physical proximity, words, or intellectual understanding. It is a "waking up" in the student's own field of consciousness to their blissful immortal essence. It's not a transmission per se but an "elevation" of the student's individual consciousness into the realization of the communion between master and discipline as pure boundless consciousness. It's as if the Guru, by virtue of having already realized his or her own nature, pulls the student's consciousness from the individual level (*jiva*) into the Guru's universal level (*shiva*). This is *shaktipat*, and it awakens an intense desire for enlightenment in the disciple.

Shaktipat is a glimpse into eternal bliss; it's an "experience" of timelessness, of the ocean of Oneness, a descending of divine energy. Does this require initiation by a physical guru? It definitely helps—if the Guru is the real deal—but it's not an absolute requirement. The real Guru is not a person but the underlying universal consciousness that can manifest through *any* form or medium, neither limited by time nor space. Even reading a simple yet profound quote or teaching can trigger such a powerful glimpse into one's nature.

Furthermore, the concept of shaktipat in most ancient traditions, is that it always comes from God—never from a person. It is not something "given by" the Guru; the Guru is just the one who helps the seeker open their "inner door" to be able to receive it.

The actual Guru is the light of your own consciousness that reveals itself to you in whatever form is the best for you at a determined moment on your path. The Guru should not be downgraded or institutionalized into an entity or person because, besides instantly limiting what a Guru actually is, this also reduces the potential impact in freeing the seeker from their personhood.

Perverting the Guru by projecting them as a person—something which is viewed as being outside of ourselves—shifts the focus from our inner realm into pure devotion for a "sacred person." This can make us dependent on the authority of an external royal guru-person, while downplaying the importance of the inner Guru. Some contemporary tantric teachings fall under this precept.

Furthermore, in countless "spiritual" communities, this has given rise to a cult of personality, backed by the financial and devotional kindness of the disciplines. This support isn't unjustified because, after all, the Guru has to eat, have access to good healthcare, and be able to afford a place to live. Additionally, the help and devotion of the disciples can help to promulgate uplifting and transformational teachings. The main issue of concern is that many of those communities are led by an ego-driven person who has hijacked the word and role of a Guru, instead of by a real Guru.

The power of a true master is both within and beyond each and every seeker, and can never be compartmentalized into an institution. An institution can serve as a means to propagate the teachings and power of a Guru, as long as everyone there recognizes that the real Guru is within each one of them. In-person access to a genuine Guru can be life-changing, but to believe it's the only way is very limiting.

"If you observe awareness steadily, this awareness itself as Guru will reveal the Truth."

- RAMANA MAHARSHI,
THE GARLAND OF GURU'S SAYINGS

"Self is the one and only Guru."

- LAHIRI MAHASAYA,
SPIRITUAL COMMENTARY ON KABIR

"Your own self is your ultimate teacher. The outer teacher is merely a milestone. It is only your inner teacher, that will walk with you to the goal, for he is the goal."

- NISARGADATTA MAHARAJ,
I AM THAT

"There is no other teacher but your own soul."

- SWAMI VIVEKANANDA,
THE COMPLETE WORKS OF SWAMI VIVEKANANDA

There should be no doubt that the real Guru is within; the outside Guru's job is to point and guide you toward the inner Guru.

At the beginning of your path, the Guru might have a form. It might appear as your personal God or Ishta Devata, as a physical guru, or even as words that serve as direct pointers; but in essence, the Guru is not a form. When you realize the emptiness of forms, you will recognize that it is the consciousness behind forms that is God, the true Guru.

Your current consciousness, which we can call human consciousness, is a single ray of light (among many) from the sun of pure consciousness. This human consciousness isn't unbroken because it falls whenever we fall asleep, giving rise to dream consciousness[2] and no apparent consciousness at all (deep dreamless sleep).

However, there is a continuity "behind" human consciousness; there is a substratum consciousness that has no name, no age, no form, and no identity; it doesn't belong to anyone, nor is it located in any place. It is unmanifested. This unbroken consciousness is infinite because it neither starts nor ends: it is outside of time. The discovery of this pure

---

[2] Refer to "Lucid Dreaming: The Path of Non-Dual Yoga" for more information regarding dreams and dream consciousness.

consciousness is the core of all spirituality, and its realization and subsequent "integration" is the manifestation of perfect fulfillment. The tantric shaktipat occurs when the awareness of being pure consciousness is brought to light within the conscious awareness of the experiencer. It is memorable.

The truth of the matter is that everything is one limitless consciousness[3]. In the process of knowing itself, this consciousness allows itself to forget who it is, so to speak, and thereby undergoes self-forgetfulness. Due to this, it seems to be differentiated into a duality, creating a subject and an object. Contracting into a limited being, it forms the "I-ego," which then limits itself even further by identifying with the physical vehicle (and even with objects, sometimes), creating friction and tension (i.e., suffering, misery, unhappiness, restlessness). Thus, the process of spirituality is one

---

[3] There is nothing outside of the field of pure consciousness. Nobody can demonstrate that anything exists without awareness being there first; physical objects, living beings, thoughts, dreams, emotions, feelings, mystic experiences, wormholes, and even the Big Bang itself—they all occur within the space of consciousness and require a consciousness so that we can even pose or acknowledge their existence. Science can't validate consciousness as an object because science itself occurs within consciousness. Nothing can escape consciousness. Even nothingness or emptiness require an awareness to be known (and a dualistic knowledge of everythingness and fullness to contrast them with). Awareness or pure consciousness—which in this book are two words for the same principle—is verily God.

of realizing the plenitude of your true essence as the transpersonal nondual and bodiless blissful consciousness, by dropping all of your false layers (i.e., misidentifications) that appear to block this ecstatic realization and allowing its perfume to progressively integrate into your dual existence.

This perfume of being, as a natural dualistic consequence of your nonconceptual Self-realization, establishes a powerful ground of being where, at all times, indivisibleness and wholeness permeate your core of existence, encompassing an expansion of the "I" into a "transcendental-I" of which a permanent current of joy, love, and peace infuse into your life. Duality is interconnected as a unified field of experience.

You are the very means by which pure consciousness awakens to itself. Without duality, there would not be ignorance, and therefore, consciousness wouldn't be able to rediscover and recognize its true nature, because it would have never forgotten it in the first place.

The self-luminous essence of pure consciousness is our nature, the subjectivity of our very being. This inner initiation into its sweet divine honey brings the subjectivity from the background into the foreground of our conscious awareness. Once we "touch" our core, we will go "back" to it over and over again, bathing in the perfume of pure consciousness until the onion-like layers of our ego, those that prevent the full realization of this truth, are shed once and for all. This is spiritual practice, and shaktipat marks the real beginning of it. Up until this Self-recognition, we are merely in the "pre-school" of the path, waiting to get ready to truly go all the way. Once the unbroken continuum shines as the never-ending sunrise, we are indeed infusing the world of forms with the light of God Himself.

CHAPTER 4

JUST ROAMING AROUND PLANET EARTH

"You are not your body. Your body is not you."

- ASHTAVAKRA GITA

"I" is the most used word in the world. Everyone says "I" every day, regardless of their culture, language, social status, or financial wealth. "I" is the universal element between every single person on this planet. After all, despite whatever name you might have, you refer to yourself, first and foremost, as "I"—"I am sleepy," "I am hungry," "I am intelligent," "I am meditating," "I am a woman," "I am Jewish," " I am African American," and so on.

"I" poses a sense of self—and what do you identify it with? Whenever you say "I," what are you referring to?

There are two main layers of identification on the spiritual path: the body (which is not limited to the physical body) and pure consciousness. The first is an identification with ignorance (although the degrees of ignorance may vary); the latter is with realization[4].

1) I = Body

I = Objects and material possessions;
I = Physical body and its attributes;
I = Mental content, thoughts, identity, and personality;
I = Life-force, energy body, subtle body, emotions, feelings.

2) I = Pure Consciousness

Most human beings erroneously identify themselves as the physical body; e.g., "The body is who I am, and when it dies, I die" or "Look at me here in this picture!"

This type of misidentification is based on the belief "I am the body." But is this belief actually true? When you hurt some

---

[4] Although someone may affirm knowing that they're not the physical body and/or mind, unless that has been their direct experience, it's just intellectual knowledge. Although this is a start, it's still not enough to disidentify from thinking one is their body in some aspect of its multilayered dimension (regardless of whether it's a subtle or gross identification).

part of your body, you say, "My [insert body part here] hurts." I.e., "My neck hurts," "My elbow aches," "My head is killing me." Sometimes, you can also say, "I [the body] am in pain."

Are you your body? Is "I" = physical body? Is your sense of self defined by your physicality?

You can say "I" when talking about the body, such as "I am thin," but you can also talk about the body as "it," such as "My body's temperature is really high."

What do we, as human beings, even mean when we say, "I am the body"? If we have hair and then shave it off, did something happen to us? Do we still feel "I am the body"? Yes, of course.

Ok, then we are not the "hair," right?

What about our limbs? What if someone has to have their leg amputated? Did something happen to that person? Yes, they lost a leg, but does that person still feel "I am the body"? Yes?

Ok, so then we are not the leg either, or any other limbs for that matter.

Are we the heart? If our heart stops beating, the body dies, right? So, whenever we feel "I am the body," are we talking about the heart? What about the lungs? Ok, so there are some critical parts without which our body just cannot continue living.

Do we think that we are the heart, the lungs, or the brain whenever we feel "I am the body"? Nobody would say so.

Therefore, what are we really expressing with the belief "I am the body"? Perhaps it feels like we are "something" that lives "inside" the physical body?

What is the "physical body," anyway? Except for our head, we can see the whole body with our eyes, which are themselves part of it. We can only see our head in a reflection. Perhaps we can see our nose, eyebrows, lips, or cheekbones, but no one ever saw their forehead or eyes without looking at a reflection.

We can also use our hands, arms, feet, and legs, which themselves are part of the physical body, to touch it. We use the tactile sense for that, which provides us with physical sensations of the skin, lips, hair, and so on. Additionally, we also utilize the proprioceptive sense to know where our limbs are in space.

So, what we know about the physical body through our direct experience so far, is that it is something that we partially see (that we can touch with other parts of the body itself) that seems to be separated from everything else, which we can call "what-is-not our body," or that some people may call "not-I." There are also lots of things that the physical body can do, such as inhaling or exhaling air, ingesting or swallowing, excreting matter, etc. What else?

40

Science says that our bodies are composed of about 55-65% water. Do we feel like a "water body"? Nobody would say so. We're trying to decipher what the feeling "I am the body" means rather than scientifically understanding what the body is composed of or its mechanisms.

What else is the feeling "I am the body" composed of? Sensations? Yes. Whatever we feel inside (feelings, emotions, etc.), these are only sensations that we perceive. Some sensations can be quite powerful, like the sensation of being localized inside the body, and even more prevalent, the sensation that our awareness is emanating from the inside of our head as if the head were the headquarters of our experience of being a body.

Are thoughts considered part of the "I am the body" experience? If so, where are they? In the head? If someone were to open your skull, would they find your thoughts in there? Not really. Therefore, this is just another layer of sensation, the sensation of thoughts being localized inside our head.

On the other hand, if thoughts are not considered part of the "I am the body" experience because they are not the "body" itself, then we are not our thoughts, correct? They just arise and vanish, although sometimes they seem to drop an anchor in the sea of our mind and linger for a little longer than we'd like.

What we said for thoughts can also be applied to feelings and emotions. Sometimes they too may be felt in our head, while other times in our solar plexus, in the heart area, etc. Would anyone find emotions or feelings in these places? No, they are not "there"—they are just perceived sensations.

So what really is our body? Sensations?

What is this "something" that seems to live inside the physical body? Is it a "soul" or a "self"? It's something that is aware of perceptions, sensations, and thoughts. This "something" that is aware of all of that is not these things, but rather, it is that which is aware of them.

If we are more than just a bundle of cells structured into blood, flesh, and bones; if we are more than just a collection of beliefs, thoughts, feelings, and emotions; if we are more than just perceptions and sensations, then we have to find out what we are.

What is this "something"? Does it live inside the body? Does it die like the body, or is it even born? Where does this "something" come from? Is it a by-product of the brain, like materialistic science seems to suggest?

Is this "something"—which we can call consciousness or awareness—in the brain, which in turn is in the head, in the body, and in the world?

Believing that consciousness is a by-product of the brain is a perplexing act of logic that refutes the existence of consciousness itself. The predominant worldview assumes that the Big Bang brought about matter, which eventually evolved into the world, the body, and the brain, out of which consciousness then emerged. But can you ever confirm this? You first need consciousness to confirm or verify anything at all—which makes consciousness the primary substrate of all things.

Can you understand this critical point? Take away consciousness, and you take away everything. Are there any thoughts or ideas about the Big Bang or anything at all when there seems to be no consciousness, like when you are in deep dreamless sleep or passed out? No, there aren't. It is only when you wake up (when you seem to regain consciousness) that such thoughts, ideas, or observations can arise. This means that they are all preceded by consciousness.

The idea or concept of the Big Bang arises *in* consciousness. The existence of anything requires consciousness of that very thing to validate its relative existence. Could we ever know about the existence of anything without consciousness? All experience or knowing comes from consciousness. Nothing can ever be known or experienced without consciousness; thus, everything that is known arises *in* consciousness.

This is what you have to find out for yourself. Unraveling this mystery of our real "Self" will unveil the mystery of consciousness and God. That's why you've enrolled in this spiritual journey—to find out that you are not and have never been just a mere body roaming around planet Earth.

IDENTIFYING WITH THE UNIDENTIFIABLE

Why would you want to identify with pure consciousness? For a start, it is not hard to understand that being identified with the body will leave you prone to suffering and unhappiness. If your sense of self is dictated by the body, what happens if it suffers from a disease? You suffer. What happens if others judge you by your body? You suffer. What if you prize yourself on your intellectual ability, but with time, as the body grows old, your mental capacity is no longer as sharp as it used to be? You suffer. It's an indisputable fact that the body will age, decay, and die. There's no escaping this, and if that's all someone thinks they are, then they will not have a pleasant dualistic existence.

In addition to thinking that "I" equals the physical body, there's often a further extension of this belief—the belief that the things we own or have, are who we are. People usually equate themselves with their material possessions

("I am wealthy" or "I am what I've accomplished"), and it's obvious this predisposes them to great suffering due to the ephemeral nature of these things.

Think about an object that is very near and dear to you. Now, imagine losing that object. Does it seem like a part of you is missing? If so, that's because you've extended your identity (your sense of self) into that object. Alternatively, imagine if a friend saw that object and, without knowing how dear it was to you, said it looked ugly or that they didn't like it at all. How would you feel? If you'd feel some form of anger or hurt, this means you are a little too identified with that object or with what it represents.

It's not uncommon to have our sense of identity spread into objects. In fact, I'd go so far as to say that everyone you know probably has one object that they deem as "irreplaceable" because they've incorporated it into their identity, even if they're not aware of that.

It's okay to be fond of an object. You don't have to throw away your great grandfather's World War II medal of honor. That won't accomplish anything. What you shouldn't allow to happen is a misidentification regarding who you are. Your true Self is not an object.

Just like the physical body, your identity and personality are impermanent; they're constantly changing. The values

45

and principles that compose your sense of identity today are not the same as from 10, 20, or 30 years ago. What you stand for now is probably not the same as it was decades ago, and it will probably not be the same decades into the future. Furthermore, the way you portray or express your identity through your personality, is constantly being shaped by the world or personal events, by close friends or relatives, and by society in general. Your likes and dislikes, for example, can change relatively easily. Perhaps you didn't enjoy something 15 years ago that you enjoy now; perhaps you're holding on to something that you don't want to let go of, even though it's hindering your spiritual progression, evolution, maturity, and bringing you suffering or restlessness. Perhaps you allow the past to continue shaping who you are today and feel incapable of making new and different choices that would lead your life in a totally different direction, one that's more aligned with what you really want deep down. Or maybe, you once let yourself be defined by negative beliefs that you've now transcended.

Your behavior, mentality, emotions, temperament, etc., change with time, and when you cling to what changes, you are always bound to suffer. You simply cannot find everlasting realization in the ephemeral. If someone says, "I have changed," as in they've changed their personality due to some occurrence, experience, or event, they're still referring to the contents of their mind. A closed, shy person may now be a charismatic, outgoing, and fun person, but ultimately, that's just an attribute of their mind that changed. "I" is the same; what changed was only "shy" to "confident." This is not who we really are.

Furthermore, whenever someone is identified with the contents of their mind, always listening to its scripts, stories, plots, etc., they get enmeshed in twisted depictions of reality, believing in mental constructs that shape their way of acting, thinking, and being. This is another name for self-inflicted torture.

Now that you've been reminded of why identifying with the body and any of its dimensions is not a good decision, we shall backtrack to the question: why would you want to identify with pure consciousness? The answer is simple: because it experiences no suffering. No unhappiness. No misery. No restlessness. No death. It's your original being, wholly realized, blissful, and incomprehensibly fulfilled. It's endless peace.

Of course, you could say that all dualistic dimensions of existence are also you or a part of you, and you wouldn't be wrong; they are all within consciousness. But here's the great thing about realizing your true nature:

You can identify with pure consciousness and still experience duality to its fullest, in all of its layers. Truthfully, it's the only way to experience what duality has to offer in all of its glory. Everything—from objects to the body, thoughts, feelings, prana, mind, etc.—they're just constantly changing expressions of God (pure consciousness), which permeates and encompasses them all.

What was once transcended is now infused into your being. You realize your misidentifications with what you are not, and then you overcome these previous negations into acceptances of your dualistic existence. Tantra doesn't negate any facet of existence, from nondual to dual. Negations were merely an instrument to now reach a more profound integration.

What was once seen as "not-I" is now seen as "also-I": "I am the body, objects, thoughts, feelings, emotions, energy, prana, mind—I am everything. These are all made out of consciousness. I am pure consciousness."

Once you realize that pure consciousness is your true Self, you will have recognized that all of your other facets are merely notes of music; they come, play beautifully, and they go, while you're the whole song and the empty score that precedes it, allows it to be, and succeeds it.

In fact, pure consciousness is not something you identify with but something that you simply are. As you go deep into the rabbit hole, you will directly experience deeper layers of your self (i.e., more purified and less physically-grounded versions of "being") until there's nothing left to identify with—there's no one that can identify with anything and nothing to be identified with[5]. Then, and only then, you'll realize that your true original being is, and has always been, nondual consciousness. It is the identification with the unidentifiable.

_____

[5] Consciousness is not an object, but the ultimate subject, which in the case of having no objects to identify with (through the mind), loses its subject apparatus and remains simply as it is: nondual.

CHAPTER 5

THE LEFT-HAND PATH

Tantra is popularly categorized under two main branches: the "Left-Hand" path (*Vama M*arga) and the "Right-Hand" path (*Dakshina Marga*).

The Left-Hand path is viewed as being synonymous with heterodoxy because it diverges from the norms, customs, and ethics of standard spiritual teachings (i.e., it deviates from typical Vedic views). In essence, most people equate it with using sexuality as the means toward liberation ("tantric sex") alongside a path with disregard toward conventional morality, while they view Right-Hand Tantra as being composed of standard meditative practices, contemplation, and a *sattvic* (pure) lifestyle.

Affirming that there are countless books and workshops that propose to teach you some form of Left-Hand Tantra would be a massive understatement. However, unbeknownst to most spiritual seekers, sex as means toward liberation is seldom mentioned in ancient tantric texts. And when it is discussed, it is highly secretive, esoteric, and mostly impenetrable by even very advanced practitioners who haven't given their life to such an unorthodox path. It's like walking on thin ice with shoes made of stone.

Many of these teachings are often entirely distorted and have mostly been lost in misunderstandings, misinterpretations, and mistranslations. They usually appeal to those who are curious but not serious about embarking on a spiritual path, falling for the utopian spiritual view indirectly presented by some of the so-called "tantric gurus" of "staying wholly absorbed in the senses, world, and its pleasures, without giving a thought to self-discipline, introspection, or effort, but gaining spiritual wisdom, unfathomable bliss, and immortality at the same time."

Moreover, obscure left-handed literature is packed with cryptic and figurative words and sentences, where they don't explicitly say what a practitioner is supposed to do or what's going on (they rely heavily on secrecy), but use symbolic terms such as "tip of the jewel" (tip of the penis), "lotus" or "yoni" (vagina), "lingam" (penis), "mercury" (semen), or even "vajra entering the consort's lotus," "bodhicitta drop," or "mahamudra consort," which I'll let you figure out for yourself. Some go as far as implying the necessity of generating sexual fluids so that they could be offered in a ritual (held in cremation grounds) and ingested[6]. I don't think any authentic seeker would want to dive into such procedures.

Nonetheless, believing that seekers would be able to use sexual union as a form of "Tantra" specifically for the sake of Self-Realization (i.e., using orgasmic blissful consciousness induced by sexual intercourse in order to realize God) is delusional. This subtle path is one of the most dangerous, complex, and easier to fall from[7]. The required equanimity, concentration, passionlessness, and self-control concerning the body's natural reactions and instincts is beyond what the typical seeker or even adept possess. Furthermore, "tantric sex" with the sole purpose of liberation was historically supposed to be done with someone to whom

---

[6] Substances such as urine, feces, or phlegm, were also used by practitioners, mixed with wine to be ritually ingested. Since such type of substances is considered highly "impure," their consumption would be a sort of "proof" that the Tantra practitioner had transcended the idea that some things are pure while others are impure, embracing the insight that the divine is equally present in all things. If you were disgusted by such an idea, then that would mean that, deep down, you hadn't really integrated such wisdom, according to ancient esoteric Left Tantra literature.

[7] Unfortunately, there are also a number of people who have been abused by "gurus" that supposedly taught secret tantric practices. But that's a subject outside of the scope of this book.

you are not attracted in order to prevent the emergence of ordinary sexual drive, which would destroy the goal of the practice. All of the Tantra "retreats" or "workshops" that propose to teach Tantra to couples have actually nothing to do with the original Tantra, whose purpose is enlightenment. Their use of the word "Tantra" has an entirely different connotation and goal.

Another issue with teachings that expound on Left-Hand Tantra is that there's generally an obsessive and unnatural—almost maniacal—concern with Tantra's sexual aspects, often leading the practitioner to overlook the real depth of Tantra and its primary goal of Self-Realization. For some seekers, sexuality becomes the center of attraction on the spiritual path, and this tunnel vision can ruin the proper path toward enlightenment. It can even destroy entire spiritual communities or ashrams.

With that being said, you can use Left-Hand Tantra teachings to integrate the bliss that originated from what "standard spirituality" would consider "uncommon sources" into a means of achieving a higher state of consciousness more quickly, which would then allow you to perform a more efficient spiritual practice. Considering that sexual energy is one of the main driving forces in Creation, you can use its energy and bliss as a trance-gateway into deeper meditative levels by redirecting it into higher spiritual centers. Furthermore, you can also use the body's instinctive sexual impulses and transform them into a desire for liberation.

In spiritual traditions, it is customary to renounce the "human" in us so that we can dedicate ourselves to our "higher" or "divine" self. However, sacrificing our humanity is not the ultimate answer, as we would be denying a facet of our existence. Of course, there must be the understanding that allows us to disidentify with the ephemeral dimension of our existence (everything that is not pure consciousness), but disidentification doesn't mean repression or complete deprivation. If you want to drink liquor, eat meat and fish, and experience physical union through sexual intercourse— you can do it. There's no punishing god out there that will chastise you for that. Repression creates an internal rupture and disturbs your ability to truly repose and surrender; sooner or later, it will explode and do terrible harm. Many ascetics are plagued by sexual desires, even if they don't admit it (to themselves), which is one of the reasons they stagnate and don't reach greater spiritual heights.

Let your biological urges express naturally and in a healthy way, without luxuriating yourself in them. Tantra doesn't rule anything out—it allows you to be as free as you want. In fact, Tantra integrates. Instead of allowing the instincts to control our human experience, Tantra integrates them into our spiritual path. In time, you will naturally find the equilibrium between being human and being God. What a magical and beautiful paradox this is!

CHAPTER 6

KUNDALINI SHAKTI

Tantra cannot be successful without the awakening of the inner fire. This fire—which is called Kundalini—is an essential component of Tantra. It burns our internal pollution, purifying it by fire, illuminating and filling the chambers of our nervous system with tremendous pranic energy. It's an offering of our awareness into both the individual life-force within our body, and the cosmic Kundalini within the universe itself. This is accomplished through different tantric practices that directly tap into the dormant Kundalini energy.

But what is Kundalini exactly?

There are various definitions of Kundalini. A straightforward one is that Kundalini is the latent cosmic energy inherent in every living being. Although it is a very misunderstood phenomenon, all forms of spirituality require a Kundalini awakening. Awakening it is synonymous with the awakening of the unconscious. You can never realize your true Being unless all the unconscious parts of your illusory identity come to the surface and you recognize them to not be you.

Although many esoteric and symbolic terms are used to describe the Kundalini, we will demystify it in the simplest of ways—it is just *prana*, life-force, but a massive reservoir of it. Many people believe it is a malevolent power or something absurd like that, but how can your own life-force, that which sustains your life, be evil? Those assumptions are merely religious dogma, and we will stay away from them. Kundalini is also pictured as a sleeping serpent coiled in *Muladhara*, the Root Chakra, because some yogis have experienced it as a "powerful serpent aggressively going up," but there is no serpent anywhere; it's just a metaphor.

To better understand the relationship between prana and our body, let's use a present-day example from *Kundalini Exposed*:

"To be able to turn the lights on, do an internet search, have the fridge working, turn on a fan, air conditioning or any other electrical device, a house needs electrical power. Without it, none of those things will work. All that power is provided through high-voltage transmission lines; yet upon reaching a house, its voltage is stepped down and greatly reduced in order to prevent burnout. There the electricity travels through wires inside the walls to the outlets and switches all over the house.

Those wires are analogous to your nervous system, which is said to be composed of thousands of subtle energetic channels called *nadis*. Prana, the life-force which runs through them, can be equated with electricity. If your body (house) only requires around 500 kWh to keep going and survive, it will never improve and adapt to a higher voltage. To run a supercomputer rather than a normal laptop, your current voltage wouldn't work. Hence, we need to increase our body's pranic capacity so that we can use more life-energy.

Now imagine we went all the way back to the power plant, where the original electrical generators are, and plugged directly into that whole energetic load rather than reducing it to accommodate our house's capacity. What would happen? Our entire electrical system would fry. This example is akin to awakening the Kundalini unprepared—it's way too much energy coursing through a system that hasn't been prepared to handle such high voltage."

Through the practice of Kundalini or Kriya Yoga (among some other disciplines), we purify our nervous system first in order to be able to receive and sustain the powerful discharge of Kundalini energy. We learn how to tap into the "power plant" reservoir and awaken it, elevating the power of our consciousness from a personal and limited awareness toward universal awareness. Harnessing and awakening this energy will change your life. Not only is it the essential carriage of your journey toward enlightenment, but it is also beneficial if you just want to have a better life, free from disease, and full of vitality, energy, and joy.

The practice of Tantra, which in many variants includes numerous yogic practices, naturally purifies our system and awakens the Kundalini energy. Tantra and Kundalini always dance together. Of course, those who've been practicing a Kundalini Yoga or Kriya Yoga[8] routine for many years are more prone to make this happen, but it's available to everyone, despite their predispositions and current body/mind "system" capacity.

Shakti—which can be seen as the personification of Kundalini energy, the life-force principle that gives life to the Universe—in its "pure form" of *ananda*, can be used as a path toward God.

Tantrics are known as venerators of the feminine. Worshipping the feminine is worshipping Shakti. However, instead of

_____

[8] Refer to Kriya Yoga Exposed and Kundalini Exposed for the respective practical routines on those spiritual disciplines. I highly recommend reading these books if you want to deeply explore Kriya Yoga and Kundalini energy.

worshipping "Shakti, the deity," we worship "Shakti, the divine bliss." Nondual Tantra does this the best.

Besides being used as a representation for Kundalini, Shakti can also be regarded as a symbol for the dual, manifested, personal, immanent, and within-time Creation. On the other hand, Shiva is a symbol for the nondual, unmanifested, transpersonal, transcendent, and timeless pure consciousness, the perennial ground of everything. The recognition of our Shiva nature is the first goal of tantric practice (i.e., realizing our original nondual nature).

"Reality really cannot be divided."

- MALINI VIJAYA UTTARA TANTRA

Reality (God or Shiva) is indivisible, immutable, limitless, not-two. It transcends all experience, perception, senses, and comprehension. It is closer to you than your own body, than your own breath, than your own dreams, than your own hopes, than your own identity, and even than your own life. The Ultimate Reality is the pure empty consciousness that allows all of those to appear and disappear, which itself is nothing, everything, and none of them. It is indefinable, and every word about it is but a limited attempt at describing the unfathomable.

As an endeavor to understand Reality with our finite mind and intellect, we have to divide it into two aspects: nondual and dual, or unmanifested and manifested, or Shiva and Shakti. The cloud of Maya makes this illusory separation seem real. However, because Reality is One and indivisible, Shiva and Shakti are not different, just like fire and heat are inseparable—they are one and the same. Shiva knows Shakti as itself. They are not divided. Shiva is "static Shakti," while Shakti is "kinetic Shiva." Shiva is the ink; Shakti is the painting. Painting only exists due to the ink, but it is what makes it beautiful.

Being-Consciousness-Bliss (*Sat-Chit-Ananda*), a term often used to denote our true nature, is Shiva-Shakti. Being-Consciousness (Sat-Chit) is Shiva, while Bliss (Ananda) is Shakti. They are indivisible! Recognizing their unity is the second goal of tantric practice (i.e., infusing the realization of our nondual nature into our dual existence; bringing our Shiva nature into the realm of Shakti).

Notwithstanding a diverse multiplicity of objects and selves (i.e., the body, world, and mind) that appears to superimpose itself on the substratum of consciousness, you shall break through such illusion of Many and find the One, only to later find the One in the Many. This is the tantric path.

Part 2

FIREBENDING

Fire though not seen at first is there all the time; it becomes visible by friction; even so the Self is there all the time though unperceived by those in a state of ignorance.

- SHVETASVATARA UPANISHAD

CHAPTER 7

THE PATHWAY OF TANTRA

Tantra, without practice, is nothing but a mixture of different theories, suppositions, and speculative and grandiose affirmations. You must validate tantric teachings for yourself through your own direct experience. Without freeing the mind from the chains of matter and ego, you won't awaken to the brilliance of Spirit.

If you have practiced Kriya Yoga, Kundalini Yoga, or even different yogic practices, you know that *sadhana* is key.

Sadhana refers to a set of spiritual guidance and practices that, if correctly followed, allows seekers to liberate themselves from the illusory bondage created by the ego and to recognize their true blissful nature.

However, whenever a seeker first attempts to tackle the system of Tantra practice, they can get easily startled by all of the intricate and confusing information available. In fact, if you were to practice all of the different types of Tantric teachings, you'd require countless lifetimes. It's just impossible to learn and practice them all. There are almost as many tantric practices as there are stars in the night sky.

There are many different forms of Tantra, many of which include complex visualization techniques and methodologies. These can be unnecessarily elaborated and cumbersome to perform, possibly becoming massive distractions and distortions to the true nondual path. This intricate approach is not a path that I'd advise the vast majority of seekers to follow unless they have a particular predisposition, which is why we won't focus on it.

Tantric practices have always been shielded from distortion by the masses by lingering under a veil of secrecy. However, secrecy is not good for the development of the practitioner nor the world, nor does it encourage ego-dissolution; and it encourages the spread of myths and fantasies about Tantra, filling it with dogma.

This is not exclusive to Tantra but to all spirituality, and it is a very controversial topic. By keeping power in the hands of only a few people, seekers have to beg for the techniques and pay large sums. This is always done under the guise of "preserving the purity of the teachings."

Initially, some aspirants are keen on finding the original tantric practices, unaware that most of them were not written down. Those few that were recorded were written in a now nearly dead language, full of ancient culture-specific allegories and symbology that don't fit today's world anymore (some of them were just inscriptions carved on walls).

Eventually, they realize that they could never truly know which ones are the original. Even though such practices have supposedly been passed down from generation to generation, it's a bit like a game of Chinese Whispers/Telephone. Get any spiritual teaching and fast-forward it one thousand years, and it will look different from when it was created, especially when you consider the lack of a more enduring and non-decayable medium such as the internet. This occurs for many reasons, such as the loss of or a change in language, distortion caused by those who disseminate teachings without fully understanding them, or due to the emergence of a completely different cultural and societal setting or context.

Nonetheless, once you realize the truth and "see the big picture," you recognize that most tantric practices can work, as long as they fulfill a few specific requirements and are correctly applied, regardless of the time and tradition they came from, and the words by which they're shared.

The Tantra presented in this book has been very carefully selected to get you from the surface level of spirituality into the depths of the ocean. The aim is always to transcend suffering, recognize our nondual nature, and incorporate such blissful realization into our dual existence. And at the end of the day, this is all that matters.

Many tantric practices expounded in this book are related to yogic sadhanas because they also aim at bringing life-force from Ida and Pingala into the central canal, Sushumna[9], giving rise to a state of heightened and expanded consciousness that allows the seeker to tap into blissful emptiness. Once stabilized there, the practitioner will then be able to transition into nondual practices whose goal is to abide in that blissful objectless awareness, shedding everything that prevents oneself from achieving Self-Realization.

However, we will not approach Buddhist Tantra's way of awakening the inner fire, which is generally done by using real or imagined consorts as a form of practice, and may go as far as performing maithuna (sexual intercourse). I recommend that the vast majority of seekers bypass this sort of practice or rituals, not only because of their controversial and

---

[9] Sushumna Nadi is the central channel within the subtle body where the fire of the Kundalini energy goes through when it is awakened. It is normally closed, and we will open it by practicing. When we open it, and the Kundalini current goes through it, we go beyond the five senses and enter into higher states of consciousness. Ordinarily, the life-force flows through the subtle side channels, *Ida* and *Pingala*, located on the left and right sides of the spinal column, respectively. When it flows through Sushumna Nadi, it's always for spiritual purposes.

peculiar methodologies and highly advanced requirements, but also because they're highly dependent upon a guru/ disciple presential relationship and initiation, as well as a specific setting rarely found "out there" in the wild.

We can then see why the practical system of Tantra has been so easily misunderstood. Casting "Neo-Tantra" aside, Tantra is mainly about asanas, bandhas, visualizations, mudras, mantras, pranayama, and different forms of meditation, sometimes with some less orthodox methods imbued into the system of practice. Its purpose is to reveal the underlying blissful awareness, which is our real identity, and then "extend" the "experience" of it in order to fully experience nonduality within duality.

To reach such profundity, you'll have to "locate" or "sense" your own background of consciousness once your mind is crystalline enough. By opening the alchemical gates of discernment, together with enough pranic energy, you can pierce through the illusion of being a separate identity. First, you become conscious of consciousness within yourself, and then you become conscious of consciousness as yourself.

You go from an individual experience of phenomena into the ground awareness that makes those very phenomena. Tantra allows us to experience the full universal manifestation of pure consciousness as everythingness and nothingness, by bringing forth an expansion of our mind into a broader field of consciousness, encompassing all things as One ("I am everything"), and at the same time, recognizing their empty nature ("Everything is empty").

If you still experience yourself as an individual grounded in duality, then you can begin to dissolve such illusion through these practices, and eventually, you'll reach a higher understanding of yourself and awaken to your essence.

There are two main types of tantric methodologies that you will perform:

- Psychosomatic sadhana

These are practices that use the body and mind, most of which can go under the name of yogic sadhana by today's standards. It uses internal objects of concentration, and the body, breath, imagination, mantra, visualization, and energy are the primary tools. We will renounce any use of external objects of focus, even though they are usually prevalent in various tantric practices.

- Nondual sadhana

There's no object of concentration in these practices; the object of awareness is the very subject itself—empty consciousness. We revert our attention into itself. This is the most advanced type of tantric practice; it's not the most complicated, but is the subtlest type of practice, one that requires an awakened discernment and the ability to recognize one's sense of "I."

That being said, this "Direct Path" approach may be too big of a leap for many seekers; melting the attention on its source may currently be something that you're still unable to do. But that's okay, you'll get there.

On the other hand, if you can go right into nondual practices, then that's what you should do. However, this doesn't invalidate the use of other methodologies first in order to get the mind ready for the most direct approach. Nonetheless, you should practice according to your current spiritual maturity, understanding, and level. Each practice leads to a subtler type of practice until you reach the level of subject-based sadhana.

Naturally, tantric teachings incorporate not only spiritual practices but also "direct pointer" contemplations (which this book is filled with) that make your mind revert to its natural state. Besides serving as guidance and instructions, this was also the intention of many tantric scriptures and oral teachings. Furthermore, countless daily activities can also be transformed into a tantric practice, given you have sufficient awareness to "tap" into and "extend" the recognition of your original blissful nature while you perform them. Washing your car, preparing a meal, taking out the trash, walking the dog, or vacuuming the house can go from being quite tedious into a calm, meditative ambiance.

Besides all of this, you will also learn how to transmute desires into spiritual hunger, redirect instinctual forces into spiritual energy, and eliminate the boundaries of the physical body by learning how to actively embody the realization of your true nature into your physical and subtle vehicles. The exploration and transmutation of the experience of the body and senses culminates in spiritual immanence. This is a Tantra special.

The teachings in this book, just like the practical methods themselves, will illuminate your mind with a steady cultivation of understanding as well as propel you to sudden new heights of previously inaccessible insight. The Tantric view, teachings, and passages from this book or other genuine tantric books or teachings, have the power to deconstruct your mental blockages, and give you powerful insights into your true nature (i.e., they reshape your mind into having more sattvic behavior, thereby making it a more fertile soil for the perennial tree of Self-Realization). If practices are Yin, then contemplating the teachings are Yang—they are interconnected. Saturate yourself in them, and you may momentarily taste the nonconceptual experience of the bliss of being!

CHAPTER 8

GUNPOWDER, CHARCOAL, AND COAL

"The purely self-illuminating truth is nothing like a cognitive process; one can become that self-illuminating truth instantaneously."

- KULARNAVA TANTRA,
EDITED BY ARTHUR AVALON

Despite sadhana, the fastest way to be Self-Realized is through the Supreme Direct Recognition. This is when, just by hearing, reading, or reflecting on the Truth, the seeker awakens to their essence of awareness.

There's no practice or method required because, after all, you are already what you seek. Pure consciousness is already what it has always been, and no ignorance can obscure it. There's nothing besides consciousness, so there's nothing to realize—it's simply impossible to be separated from That.

However, saying that this approach won't work for 99.99% of seekers would be an understatement. Many of today's teachers approach spirituality through the lens of "No goal, no awakening, no practice, and no technique, nothing to do, nothing to accomplish, you are already the Self," which can cause immense harm to sincere seekers.

> "If you sit at home and say: 'I want to pass an exam,' nothing will happen. You have to undertake the necessary steps. Similarly, you have to take the road that leads to peace."
>
> - SRI ANANDAMAYI MA,
> AS THE FLOWER SHEDS ITS FRAGRANCE

As it's written in Turiya—The God State:

> "If you follow this type of *Neo-Advaita* teaching, from either the "nothing to do" or the "you are already enlightened" school, you will go nowhere. At best, you will stagnate in a tiny "peace-empty" feeling after doing 5 minutes of intellectual Self-inquiry, and then you'll believe that you are enlightened, especially if the teacher or guru says "Yes, that is the Self! You have awakened!" Then you can become a guru too.

In all seriousness, the aforementioned is what's trending nowadays. It may have its purpose in certain circumstances, but it is mostly deceiving and unhelpful. All genuine and truthful Gurus, such as the Buddha, Lahiri Mahasaya, and Ramana Maharshi preached the importance of spiritual practice."

Some seekers foolishly believe they've become enlightened as a result of some experience they've had. Sometimes, this comes together with the messiah complex. Despite how hurt the ego can become, it's best to put aside any beliefs that "I am the chosen one" or "I am enlightened." Almost everyone requires some sort of practice to realize their true Self. This leads us to tantric practice.

You have to truthfully assess which level you currently are at (this is where a genuine presential guru or competent teacher may be helpful). Then, you will do the practices according to your current level of spiritual progress and maturity. In case of doubt, you can always start from the very beginning and progress your way up. But it may also depend on what type of spiritual seeker you are.

There are three types of seekers:

Some are like gunpowder, which can quickly go from body-mind sadhanas into nondual sadhana (their sadhana explodes quickly[10]). They're ripe for realization and have most likely been practicing for many lifetimes. This type of seeker is extremely rare.

Some are like charcoal, and they take a short time to get ignited. They will progressively go from one level to a deeper one. This occurs during one lifetime, but it may take decades.

And finally, there are the "coal seekers," who take a long time to progress into deeper stages. Perhaps this is their first lifetime attempting spiritual practices. They shouldn't be discouraged because nobody knows whether they're "coal," "charcoal," or "gunpowder" seekers. Beginners can be a "gunpowder seeker," and so can advanced students.

How can an advanced student, who has been practicing for many years in this lifetime, be considered a "gunpowder seeker"? Perhaps they've been doing the wrong practices, receiving inadequate guidance, or some unrecognized blockage is preventing them from the explosive spiritual evolution they potentially have. Those who affirm that they "see nothing, feel nothing, experience nothing" may also be "charcoal seekers" for the same reasons as mentioned above.

---

[10] This doesn't mean that the "gunpowder seeker" will instantly go into nondual practice. By "quickly," I don't mean two weeks, but 6-12 months to a few years of intense sadhana.

The tantric sadhana laid out in this book follows a natural progression from psychosomatic practices (beginner, subject-object practices) up to direct nondual practices (subject-only practice). It is understandable because rare are those who are incarnated here and have almost no spiritual work to do at all. We all have and come with some baggage that we have to live through, purify, and transcend. Therefore, the practice of reposing in consciousness as consciousness and melting the last subtle remains of misidentification and karmic imprints are best left to when we are genuinely spiritually mature and capable of diving into the empty vacuum of transpersonal consciousness.

Nonetheless, Tantra considers that the realization must be on the body, energy, and mind level. Realizing who you truly are (the separate "I" loses its boundaries and realizes its true boundless nature) is synonymous with the mind awakening to its pure consciousness nature. However, then, your body, its energy, and your experience of duality itself must reflect such realization. You can realize your true nature and essence, yet it may happen that your body/energy may still be "catching" up to such illumination. There's still some lingering smoke, even after the mayic bonfire has been extinguished. Often, the situation is that the smoke naturally disappears with time as you remain centered in yourself; or you realize that your body and its energy are just

77

dualistic, ephemeral, and illusory dream-like contents, and they don't bother you, nor does it really matter how they currently are because you're not identified with them. Their "dualistic heaviness" fades, and they get more transparent over time, such that you never need to give them a second thought. Many great masters disregard their dualistic exist-ence, and there's nothing wrong with that. It's just how it is.

But Tantra favors the path of integration. So, after turning away from the contents of experience and awakening to one's true nature of empty blissful consciousness, you shift toward the experience of the body and its energy in order to actively melt its smoke-like boundaries, assimilating realization into these grosser dimensions. This is the integrative phase of Tantra, where the experience of duality composed of percep-tions and sensations flourishes as luminous awareness itself.

CHAPTER 9

TANTRIC PURIFICATION

The spiritual practices of Tantra have the purpose of purifying your mind to make it translucent so that it can allow the light of consciousness to shine through more easily. When your psyche is full of mental constructs, patterns, and blockages, you cannot recognize the imperishable background of consciousness, just like a fish in water doesn't recognize that it's within the water. Whatever type of tantric practice you perform, this type of purification is a *must* as a form of preparation.

Typically, every single content that appears in our conscious mind is interpreted and attributed a meaning that makes sense to the ego's self-created concept of itself. If something conflicts with the ego's story (with our "false self" story), the ego will either deem it irrelevant and ignore it (allowing it to barely reach the conscious mind), or will interpret it in a way that fits the ego's identity, composing a logical story (from the ego's perspective) so that the ego's reign remains unaffected.

All of the things that the ego doesn't want to accept and integrate into its narrative (because they would destroy its foundations), or that the ego ignores due to pain, fear of suffering, or just because it's not coherent with its identity, are stored beneath the conscious mind in the subconscious. These accumulated traumas, suffering, and delusions greatly affect the flow of prana within the subtle body.

The subtle body is the link between matter and consciousness, and the more inner pollution that you have stored there, the stronger you feel that you are an entity who is limited, time-bound, and prone-to-suffering.

Contrary to popular belief, our mind is not wholly in the head but rather is spread out through the body through the nervous system and brain (nadis and chakras), sometimes even expanding beyond it. Traumas, fears, and all emotional contractions and repressions are stored in the appropriate energetic place within the subtle body. Even small things like a foot massage or practicing some specific asanas, if done correctly, can release stored up emotional stressors, bringing some relief.

Whenever we do spiritual practice, we are purifying both the conscious and the subconscious by increasing the power of our life-force, discernment, wisdom, concentration, mind-fulness, awareness, and lucidity. By bringing the subconscious mental constructs, patterns, and blockages up to the conscious mind, they can be seen with the eyes of wisdom and realized as not-self. The recognition that they belong to a temporary identity created by a false "I" diminishes the power they have over us by gradually diminishing our attachment to them until they disappear entirely.

Whenever we perform a practice that emphasizes the Third-Eye (Ajna Chakra, the seat of the conscious mind), it is because we want to bring all the subconscious debris (which are spread out via prana through the whole body-mind system in the nadis and chakras, often manifested as a "web" of sensations, emotions, feelings, etc.) into the conscious mind (Ajna Chakra). In Tantra, we can use this process to purify and bring each chakra's stored *samskaras*[11] up to the Third-Eye, where they can be seen and purified for what they are.

There are many knots in the subtle body, some stronger, some subtler. They must be untied to allow the life-force to flow more smoothly through the nadis, otherwise, they will keep your system tense and block further progress. Many of

---

[11] *Samskaras* is a word that denotes unconscious tendencies, subtle habits and desires, psychological imprints, mental impressions, or deep-buried emotional traumas.

these knots are energetic and emotional blockages reinforced by negative experiences and impressions, and they create a firm obstruction to the movement of the life-force. Both body-mind and nondual practices gradually untie them, making all the stored up latent impressions come to the surface so that you can erase them.

You begin by doing the obvious: relaxing the body and mind through the practice of asanas (yogic postures), followed by a complete slowdown induced by deep and controlled calm breathing. Then you focus all of your attention on a specific chakra-point, falling into an even deeper, more peaceful state of consciousness, thereby expanding your conscious mind. As your conscious mind expands and connects with the subconscious, you begin to tap into the chakra's subtle energy, untangling some energetic pressure off the plexus and allowing samskaras to be "brought up" into the light of awareness to be purified.

In these deeper states, as those samskaras that are usually lying below your conscious mind are being illuminated in the seat of the conscious mind, they can manifest as thoughts, imagery, memories, emotions, energetic surges or pressures, trembles, moans, involuntary or spontaneous movements, among other possibilities. Some of these are typically called "kriyas," and they can be physical, emotional, or mental.

It all depends on how smoothly life-force is flowing through your nadis and the type of purification that you're going through at that time.

Because you will be actively using your ability to concentrate on stirring up the pranic centers in your nervous system, you'll most likely experience a release of those samskaras through physical or emotional kriyas. Since these samskaras are primarily stored up as pranic blockages, it makes sense that their release effect will also be, in a sense, the effect that prana will have on the body (e.g., involuntary movements, shaking, or energetic pressures).

In some deeper cases (e.g., deep-buried trauma), the purification process may actually involve remembering a forgotten memory, an image that invokes deep pain, or a thought that brings sadness. However, because you'll be uplifting those very samskaras (regardless of their type of release-manifestation) into the space of your conscious mind during the practice, you will be able to witness them with much more wisdom, remaining calm, tranquil, and with equanimity. By virtue of this fresh sense of heightened awareness, you can realize that those memories, traumas, emotions, imprints, desires, etc., are "not-I" and "not mine." They are not you, and they shall not define who you are.

This whole process creates dispassion/non-attachment in you

concerning the fake "I," its personality, and all of its stories, purifying your consciousness so that it can become ripe for the self-recognition of its pure stainless nature. Often, this process doesn't occur in the way you might expect, nor will it be as fast as one would hope.

On the other hand, on some rare occasions, you can also quickly overcome it. For example, you may think that you'll experience a vision/sensations of trauma, and that you will go through them with acceptance, recognizing that such trauma doesn't belong to you but to the ego, and since the ego isn't who you are, the trauma's grip on you is reduced, and hence it just goes away and you stop identifying yourself with it. However, what often occurs is that this whole abovementioned process happens without being translated by the mind through images, thoughts, or sensations. Due to your higher state of consciousness, there's just a "flash," or a sudden "knowingness" or insight, and the weight of that issue just goes away; the chains that bind you or the story that you used to believe simply dissolve into nothingness. You let go of that blockage or negative imprint.

When we talk about chakras, it's important to understand that the "Third-Eye" or Ajna Chakra is more than just a plexus of intricate networks of nadis (subtle channels) where life-force flows. For example, the concept of "Awakening/opening the Third-Eye" is a figure of speech. What happens in these cases is that the conscious mind expands beyond its usual "waking state limits" into the subconscious mind, enabling it to access a broader range of the subtle manifestations that were previously concealed by the five senses. This allows one to consciously enter into states beyond wakefulness, which are usually confined to trance states, dreaming, hypnosis, etc. Some examples of this include having access to the collective unconscious, seeing subtle symbolic representations with the mind's eye superimposed on the waking state's physical vision, actually seeing what is being visualized or imagined, and so on.

In tantric practice, all of the unconscious parts of your illusory identity that block you from realizing its falseness will be brought to the surface[12]. This purification process is essential, as it fills the unilluminated places within you with the pure light of awareness. To purify, as the word suggests, is to be free from internal pollution. As long as there is a heavy layer of smog, you'll never see the bright blue skies of awareness—and that's why no one should ever skip this critical step.

---

[12] When it is written that all the unconscious parts are brought to the conscious mind, this is meant in relation to enlightenment. It does not imply that realizing your true nature will give you access to and control over your digestive process, immune system, or metabolic rate. It can, but it probably won't. For these processes to be brought up to the conscious mind, they do require different yogic practices. This explanation should, therefore, not be taken out of context.

CHAPTER 10

TANTRIC SADHANA

"Sadhana is but a persistent attempt to cross over from the verbal to the non-verbal. The task seems hopeless until suddenly all becomes clear and simple and so wonderfully easy."

- NISARGADATTA,
I AM THAT

A restless mind. This is what the vast majority of seekers find when they attempt to do spiritual practice for the first time. The mind is restless because that's the habit it has cultivated; it's just reaping the fruits it sowed.

Achieving a calm state of mind is a necessity; it lays out the fertile soil for transcendence. Without a calm mind, nothing can be accomplished in Tantra. There are many ways to calm the mind but relaxing the body and slowing the breathing are two of the greatest methods. Asana (yogic posture), Bandha (yogic lock), and Pranayama (restraining the life-force; controlling the breathing process) are some of the best methods that you can use to get the mind into a relaxed, calm state.

The following introductory practices are not mandatory. There are countless methods to bring the body and mind into a meditative state of flow. If you already have a regular spiritual routine, you can keep performing it and then try the later, more powerful tantric exercises to see if they fit with your sadhana, temperament, and predisposition.

BODY

First of all, you need to have a relaxed body and a tranquil state of mind. It can be as simple as sitting down because of your body-mind's previous conditioning from all the spiritual practices you've done throughout your life. This means that by merely sitting down, your whole system slows down, and you become extremely relaxed and calm but alert. Then you are ready to go to the actual practices.

If this is not possible, I suggest you practice a few yogic postures to relax the body and mind and tranquilize the nervous system, improving the flow of prana.

Through asanas, we are doing something very simple that helps prepare the body/mind for further spiritual practice. I suggest you do these four yogic postures; they're relatively straightforward. But if you can perform any yogic posture, as long as it relaxes your body and calms your mind.

1- Vajrasana (kneeling seat)

Stay in this position for around 30 seconds.

2- Paschimottanasana (seated forward bend with each leg and then both legs at the same time)

Do each pose for 30 seconds. Try to bend at your waist rather than bending your back; it's okay if the leg isn't fully stretched or straight at the knee.

3- Uttanasana (standing forward bend)

Hold this position for 30 seconds without forcing anything at all. It's okay if the legs aren't fully stretched. Just make sure you do it carefully and don't hurt your back. There's no need to do it perfectly; you merely want to get your body and nervous system looser and more relaxed.

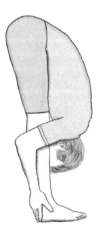

4- Anuvittasana (standing backbend)

Hold this position without forcing anything at all for 5 seconds each time. Watch out for your lower back, don't stretch your body over your current ability. You can squeeze your glutes if it helps. Do it 3-5 times.

Perform this 4-step asana cycle three times. It shouldn't take more than 10 minutes.

BREATH

To further slow down your mind and energetically warm up your subtle body/nervous system, you'll need to perform some type of practice where the breath functions as the main object of concentration. Pranayama does this wonderfully. Although pranayama can be the bread and butter of your sadhana, here we'll use it as a form of preparation for an even more potent tantric practice.

In this practice, you will perform Nadi Shodhana Pranayama (also known as alternate nostril breathing). This is done by closing off one nostril with a finger and inhaling through the other one for a specific amount of time; then exhaling in reverse by opening the closed nostril and closing the opened one for another amount of time. There are also pauses after inhaling (*Antar Kumbhaka*) and after exhaling (*Bahya Kumbhaka*), which can be held for different lengths of time. There are countless variations of this technique, but since we want to use it as a preparation to still the mind, balance the life-force, and warm up the subtle body, we'll use an uncomplicated yet efficient version:

1- Sit down cross-legged or on a chair, and exhale fully.

2- Use the thumb of the right hand to gently close the right nostril.

3- Inhale through the left nostril for a count of five. You can count "One, two, three, four, five" in your native language. You can also mentally chant "Om" five times instead if you prefer.

4- Close both nostrils after the inhalation and pause for a count of five. Since you already have the right nostril closed, all you have to do is to use the right ring finger to close the left nostril.

5- After the pause, unblock the right nostril (while still keeping the left nostril closed) and slowly exhale completely through it.

6- Close both nostrils after the exhalation and pause for a count of five yet again. Since you already have the left nostril closed, all you have to do is to use the thumb of the right hand to close the right nostril.

7- After the pause, unblock only the right nostril and inhale for a count of five while keeping the left nostril closed.

8- Close both nostrils after the inhalation and pause for a count of five. Since you already have the left nostril closed, all you have to do is to use the right thumb to close the right nostril.

9- After the pause, unblock the left nostril and exhale completely through it.

This is one round. To do multiple rounds, after step 9, go back to step 3 and continue from there.

Do multiple rounds for around 10 minutes. If you feel like you want to make this technique more potent, increase the length of the pauses to eight seconds.

Always maintain a straight back as comfortably as possible. The back, neck, and head should be in alignment.

Once ten minutes of this exercise are enough to achieve a reasonable degree of mental stillness and help you to connect better with the subtle body, you can proceed to the main technique.

ENERGY

In this section, you will learn how to connect with each chakra and how to perform tantric purification, as explained in chapter 9, "Tantric Purification." If you've prepared your body and mind correctly by performing yogic postures and some form of pranayama, your current state will be deeper than regular waking consciousness. This is essential because if your consciousness is too anchored into physicality and the grosser senses, it will be difficult to feel the subtle energetic centers, activate them, and release samskaras.

You should use a japamala to count the number of rounds on each chakra during this practice. Alternatively, you can do it by programming a timer, but in the beginning, it's best if you use a mala so that each chakra gets the same number of rounds, time, and attention.

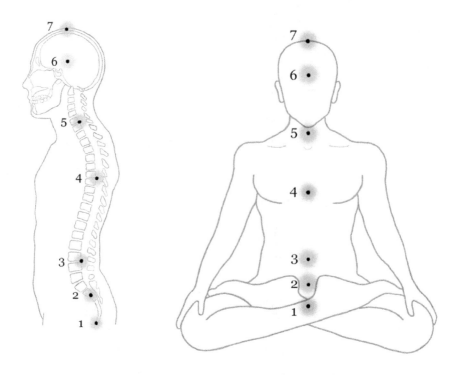

1. Muladhara (Root Chakra)

2. Swadhisthana (Sacral Chakra)

3. Manipura (Navel or Solar Plexus Chakra)

4. Anahata (Heart Chakra)

5. Vishuddha (Throat Chakra)

6. Ajna (Brow or Third Eye Chakra)

7. Sahasrara (Crown Chakra)

Look at a picture of the seven main chakras and try to locate them within your subtle body, one at a time, by using your attention to find their right spot within your spinal cord. You'll know you've found a chakra when by placing your attention onto the exact area where the chakra is supposed to be located, you feel a "sweet pressure," subtle heat, or a sort of tingling or numbness. Of course, each chakra may give you different sensations, but at the bare minimum, you should experience some version of these three types of sensations. There are many chakras within the subtle body, but we'll only focus on these seven, so make sure your attention is as close as possible to the chakra's location, as shown in the picture. With time, you'll be capable of locating and tapping into each chakra instantly.

Most practitioners focus on a point along the body's surface, either in the front or the back of the body, and directly in line with the position of the chakra. Initially, you can do this to get a feeling for the chakra's position within Sushumna Nadi, but you'll have to focus on the precise plexus where the subtle center is located during the practice, instead of its skin surface point.

The mantra used during this practice will be "Om." Mantras are powerful tools in Tantra. They've been used in spiritual practice for thousands of years due to their ease of use and efficacy in producing tangible results. Their repetition increases concentration, relaxes the mind, and gives rise to a higher state of consciousness, among other more radical possibilities. Many spiritual schools employ mantra as the main practice, but here, you will use it as a tool to purify the subtle body and to enliven your perception of your subtle centers and their respective energy.

When your mind uses a mantra as the vehicle to enhance your focus "point of attention," energy begins to stir and "wake up" from its dormant state. Using a mantra is like using a powerful shovel to dig up the soil of your subconscious mind, removing buried pollution, but also discovering precious treasures.

INSTRUCTIONS

1- Focus on Muladhara (Root Chakra).

2- Once you are clearly focusing on the chakra, begin chanting Om into the chakra. This can be done by "placing" the mantra into the chakra itself for around 5 seconds. Each time you chant Om into the chakra, you will feel a subtle vibration within the chakra, which is the effect of the Om. You can visualize an intense light appearing within the chakra each time you chant it into the chakra. It will then disappear once the mantra fades off. Perform this step for around half a mala (54 beads; put something to mark the middle of the mala so that you know you've reached its middle) or 5 minutes. There will be some energy release from the plexus and some built-up energy around it as well.

At some point, you will naturally feel drawn to stay silent and perform the mantra mentally instead of vocally. This can happen during the practice itself or after many sessions.

3- Now, gently raise the built-up energy through Sushumna Nadi, via the center of your spinal cord, until the Ajna chakra in the middle of the head. You can visualize a bright light going upward toward the brain. With time and practice, you'll be able to do this better. To move the energy, use your attention as if it were a "point of awareness," moving it from the chakra where it was, up the Sushumna Nadi, until it reaches the Ajna Chakra, in the middle of your head.

As the energy goes up, it will pass through each chakra, and you may feel or experience different sensations. For example, you may experience some extra tingling pressure, some ecstatic current, or something like a sudden "spinal goose-bump," among dozens of other possible effects.

4- Once it reaches the Ajna Chakra, let it dwell there for around a minute or so. It doesn't have to be precisely one minute; do it for the amount of time you feel a minute takes.

5- Then, let all of the energy explode upward as light through Sahasrara (Crown Chakra) on the top of the head. As you do this, roll your eyes upward, comfortably, as if you were attempting to look at the ceiling. Do not move your head, and don't attempt to close your eyes; let them be semi-opened. They might blink a lot at the beginning, but with practice, it will become natural. Just don't strain them. This is a very potent form of *Shambhavi Mudra*.

6- Repeat this process for the remaining four chakras: Swadhisthana (Sacral Chakra), Manipura (Navel or Solar Plexus Chakra, in the spine at the level of the navel), Anahata (Heart Chakra), and Vishuddha (Throat Chakra).

This whole practice should take around 25 minutes and no more than 30.

At any point throughout this practice, because of the purification involved and since we're engaging with five different subtle centers, the release of samskaras may manifest in myriad ways. Besides the various sensations and effects already described, you may also experience dream-like visions, old memories, or strange thoughts, and you may feel a strong emotional release. The effects that you'll experience will be commensurate with the current state of your body and mind, the type of imprints that you're purifying, and your spiritual maturity.

As you free yourself from energetic and emotional block-ages, the flow of life-force within your subtle body will become much smoother, allowing you to more easily tap into the potency of your inner fire.

THE WAY OF BLISS

In many forms of Tantra, worship, devotion, and union with deities play a crucial role. Such practices have the ultimate purpose of uniting the practitioner with a deity. By uniting with the chosen deity, the practitioner would acquire the deity's wisdom, characteristics, and illumination. In deeper yet rarer forms of Tantra, the end goal is not to unite with the deity or guru per se but to realize that their essence and your essence are the same nondual pristine consciousness.

However, I'm not an advocate of tantric practices that place so much emphasis on deity unification as the means of achieving "enlightenment." In my view, anything that dwells too much on form and duality is not optimal for enlighten-ment, and it can become a blockage down the road—when the practitioner has to "tackle" empty consciousness directly, which is an inescapable step if you want to realize your true nondual essence. This occurs due to residual impressions leftover from such practices. As always, though, it will depend on the seeker's predispositions, cultural background, and spiritual temperament.

Taking this into consideration, however, there's something invaluable in uniting with a deity for those who are on a more direct path toward enlightenment—if that deity is *bliss*.

Deity typically means "divine entity," "god/goddess," or refers to a "supernatural being" that interacts with humans and is capable of uplifting their consciousness to higher levels. However, the word *deity* originally meant "divine nature," which comes from the Latin word *Deus*, meaning God. Well, what's the "divine nature" of God? It is bliss. God is the pinnacle of happiness. I want to clarify that God is not an entity or a form; that would make God limited by your perception and consciousness. God is formless; it is your own consciousness. The difference is that your consciousness appears to be limited (ego-consciousness), while God is infinite consciousness.

"Ever-new Joy is God. He is inexhaustible."

- Sri Yukteswar Giri,
Autobiography of a Yogi

In the following tantric practice, called *Tantric Fire*, you will invite bliss to a dance, awakening your inner fire and rising your life-force into the higher subtle centers. Through this method, you will merge with the deity known as "bliss" by going on its chariot toward the heavens. This deity has no form, age, or personality. It's just transpersonal bliss—the divine nature of consciousness. Instead of representing a deity through a yantra[13] and using it as the medium of connection, you will directly invoke the deity (bliss) within yourself.

This tantric method uses the breath, *kumbhaka* (breath-retention), prana, *bandhas* (yogic locks), Kundalini energy, and bliss. It can be done in the standard meditative way (sitting with the eyes closed), but also in other less orthodox ways (depending on how you invoke bliss). Bliss is always its main catalyst, regardless of the method used, and there are many ways of inducing it.

In the context of this book, used as a sitting practice, this technique should be done after the practice from the previous chapter.

---

[13] Yantra is a mystic or symbolic image/diagram used for spiritual practice, traditionally used for worshipping deities or in tantric rituals. It is said that most of the time, they're used to attain siddhis or to fulfill one's desires. If the practitioner's maturity is more spiritually elevated, yantras can also be used for spiritual liberation.

In this technique, you will have to invoke the feeling of bliss in the space of the heart, which, together with breath restraint, comprises the essence of the technique[14]. Since invoking bliss is a prerequisite, you'll have to achieve this before successfully employing the technique.

Invoking bliss will function as a bridge in order to allow you to easily tap into your natural and inherent limitless bliss— the one that doesn't require any external event to be experienced. Such bliss has the power to overcome and dissolve suffering, leading one from the realm of duality into unity. Bliss is our fuel.

> "The shrine which consists of the ether [space] in the heart, the blissful, the highest retreat [treasure], that is our own, that is our goal, and that is the heat and brightness of the fire and the Sun."
>
> - MAITRAYANIYA UPANISHAD

---

[14] Avid practitioners of Kriya Yoga or Kundalini Yoga may attempt to perform this practice, but if things are already going well during those types of sadhanas, you should keep doing them. If you practice Kriya Supreme Fire (a powerful Kundalini-activator technique shared in *Kriya Yoga Exposed* and *Kundalini Exposed*), you can try to replace it with Tantric Fire, if after attempting it a few times, it seems to work better for you. Although they are different, they have a similar purpose and should not co-exist simultaneously during a spiritual routine. Alternatively, you can fit this practice into your routine right after you perform some form of Pranayama or breathwork.

INVOKING BLISS

What's the easiest way to invoke the feeling of bliss in your heart? You can just focus on the feelings of bliss, joy, happiness, and it may emerge. For some seekers, focusing on the heart chakra also brings up a sense of bliss and joy.

If neither of those methods work very well, there are a few other ways to achieve it, and you can try them now until you feel bliss in the space of your heart. Read this, choose a method, close your eyes, and try your best to feel and bathe in bliss in the heart-lotus for around 10 minutes. If it helps, you can place your hands on your sternum where the frontal surface point of the Heart Chakra is, with the intention of waking up a feeling of bliss (using *anjali mudra*[15] or "heart mudra[16]").

I) Recall one of the happiest moments of your life. Try to remember how you felt at that time; bring back the same joy and bliss that you experienced.

II) Think about the person(s) or being(s) that you love the most. This can be a husband, wife, son, daughter, children,

---

[15] Slight bow, hands pressed together with the palms touching, fingers pointing upwards, and thumbs gently pressing against the sternum. It's like the "Namaste" hand position but gently pressing against the sternum.

[16] The right hand rests on the sternum, gently pressing it, while the left hand rests on top of the right hand (or vice versa).

grandchildren, pet, friend(s), family, a Guru or spiritual master, or anyone that you feel a deep, joyful connection with. Invoke that blissful connection with them in your heart. Hugging someone you have a profound connection with may also give rise to a blissful feeling in the heart.

III) Contemplate and focus on what God is or means to you; what love symbolizes to you; or listen to sacred music that awakens joy in your heart.

IV) Go do something that will bring you a feeling of bliss. Whether the bliss is triggered by a more spiritually conventional or transgressive mean is up to you, as long as it's in harmony with the spiritual path you want to walk through. Once you're experiencing it, focus on it so that it doesn't fade, and come back to this exercise of dwelling on that feeling of bliss. If it evaporates too quickly, try your best to invoke those feelings of joy and happiness again that you just experienced. Remember that you're not looking for uncontrollable ecstasy, but bliss.

V) Any other method you may think of that invokes feelings of bliss in your heart, as long as it's not harmful to your body, mind, or spiritual path, and it doesn't hurt any living being. I leave this up to you.

Notice how warm feelings emerge in your heart. Invite a sense of "feeling-good" or restfulness or "at peace" in your heart. There's a euphoric calmness arising inside of you, and your heart will begin to feel embraced, as if there's some sweetness pressuring it, giving rise to a beautiful blissful feeling. Bathe in this bliss, allowing it to become more noticeable and more present. It doesn't have to be a strong feeling; it just has to be some form of bliss. Even if the feeling is subtle, it will grow and expand later on during the practice.

Keep repeating this for a few weeks until you're able to invoke the feeling of love-bliss quickly. Once you can do so, you can perform the actual practice.

BANDHAS

In this practice, you'll also use *bandhas*. Therefore, it's important to understand what they are. Bandha means "lock"—and refers to firmly but gently contracting a specific part of the body. When done correctly, this will directly affect the subtle body. These locks prevent prana from escaping, thus helping to sustain a higher level of energy that can be directed toward Sushumna Nadi. They are also potent Kundalini stimulators and can even improve blood flow and physical health by massaging the internal organs and nerves.

109

The three bandhas we will use are *Mula Bandha, Uddiyana Bandha*, and *Jalandhara Bandha*. Together they make up the *Maha Bandha*, the "Great Lock." Uddiyana Bandha and Jalandhara Bandha are easy to perform, and they will be explained during the technique itself. Maha Bandha, however, requires a stand-alone explanation:

Mula Bandha (Perineum Lock)

There are many esoteric explanations regarding Mula Bandha, but it's just a name for the contraction of the perineum, which is the area between the scrotum and the anus in males, and between the vulva and the anus in females.

It is straightforward to do. Focus on the perineum and contract the muscles there. That's it, pretty easy.

If, for some reason, you lack the mind-muscle connection to do it, do not worry. That's not a problem. You can easily accomplish it within a few days of various attempts.

To hasten this process, you can work on your pelvic muscles. Lay down on your back and pump those muscles for as long as you can while letting the rest of the body relax. After some days or weeks, you will be able to control these muscles consciously.

When sitting cross-legged, if you can press the perineum

with the heel while doing this bandha, it will help stimulate Muladhara Chakra and Sushumna itself.

In the practices explained in this book, whenever we perform Mula Bandha, we will do it together with two mudras, *Vajroli / Sahajoli Mudra* and *Ashwini Mudra,* for an even more potent effect.

Mudra means "seal." It is a gesture performed to improve the flow of the subtle energies. Despite being associated with hand gestures, they can be done with any part of the body or even the whole body.

Vajroli / Sahajoli Mudra (sexual organ contraction)

Vajroli Mudra is for men, while Sahajoli Mudra is for women. They both do the same thing, but they are slightly different since both sexes have different anatomies. I'll give you a raw and straightforward explanation of how to do them: just hold the same muscles you hold when you want to stop urinating. This sentence makes everyone quickly understand how to do it. In our case, it is okay if you can't hold the perineum and the urethral sphincter separately because we want to hold both at the same time.

Ashwini Mudra (anal contraction)

Ashwini Mudra is done by contracting the anal sphincter. Again, in this particular case, it's okay if you can't do it by itself separately since we'll be using both mudras and Mula Bandha at the same time.

With enough practice, you will be able to firmly apply Mula Bandha, Vajroli/Sahajoli Mudra, and Ashwini Mudra while you are holding your breath.

From here on and to keep things simple, whenever I refer to Mula Bandha in this book, it is actually the combination of Mula Bandha, Vajroli / Sahajoli Mudra, and Ashwini Mudra, as just explained.

Mula Bandha is also an excellent way to sublimate sexual energy and raise it to the higher centers. Whenever you feel an upsurge of sexual energy, instead of letting it dwell in the lower centers and solidify into sexual desire, you can perform Mula Bandha to elevate it and transform it into spiritual desire.

You can do this by holding Mula Bandha and then slowly inhaling and visualizing energy coming up from the bottom of the spine through the middle of the spinal cord until it reaches either Ajna or Sahasrara chakras, where you release the bandha and slowly exhale. Repeat this multiple times.

You may feel some ecstatic conductivity in the spinal cord (e.g., goosebumps or tingling).

There will come a time when doing a single Mula Bandha will activate the Kundalini energy upward, producing immense bliss from the Root to the Crown. The whole Sushumna Nadi will be ecstatically and vibrantly perceived.

TANTRIC FIRE INSTRUCTIONS

1- Touch the soft palate with your tongue and keep it there throughout the entire practice. If you can, perform Khechari Mudra[17] (as is taught in Kriya Yoga Exposed) as it will make the practice more powerful.

2- Invoke the feeling of bliss in the space of the heart. Notice the sweet pressure arising around your heart area. Focus on that feeling of bliss. Don't try to expand it outwards toward the rest of the body—let it be in the heart space.

3- Inhale up to 75-90% of full capacity, slowly pulling prana from the Root Chakra (Muladhara) toward the Heart Chakra (Anahata) through Sushumna Nadi. This pranic movement will gradually increase the bliss in your heart,

---

[17] Khechari Mudra means inserting the tongue into the hollow of the nasal pharynx.

but again, don't let the bliss expand or explode. It must stay within the heart area.

4- Once the inhalation has finished and prana has reached the heart, relax and gently hold the breath for around one minute, and focus on the bliss in the heart. Perform Mula Bandha (Perineum Lock).

5- You may experience heat and your body may begin to shake, but stay relaxed as best as you can, focusing on the feeling of bliss in your heart.

6- Release Mula Bandha and exhale, slowly pushing prana from the Heart Chakra (Anahata) toward the Root Chakra (Muladhara). You might also feel some "ecstatic electricity" going from the Root Chakra upward through the spinal column.

7- As you exhale the air out of your lungs, suck your abdomen in and upward (i.e., begin performing Uddiyana Bandha[18], the Abdominal Lock) until you're out of air.

8- Once your lungs are entirely out of air, and you're holding the contraction of Uddiyana Bandha, gently hold your breath again, and slowly bend the head forward and press

---

[18] This technique stimulates the Manipura Chakra, arousing a lot of heat and fire in that area. It will also excite the sympathetic nerves of the so-called "solar plexus region," bringing many health benefits.

the chin against the top of the sternum (i.e., perform Jalan-dhara Bandha[19]), while performing Mula Bandha at the same time. Keep all three locks in place and focus on the feeling of intense bliss in your Heart Chakra area. Keep the breath-hold for around one minute. Don't force anything. You should experience some sort of "complete centeredness" at this point, which will make your body and mind totally still and blissfully empty.

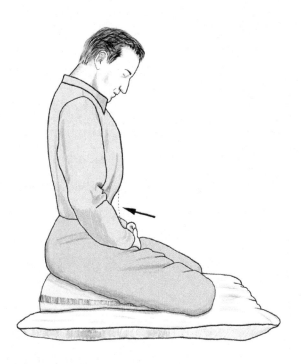

---

[19] Be careful with your neck and do this movement slowly. Make sure you have no problems with your cervical spine before attempting it. This technique stops prana from leaving the body in the throat area and often helps to improve the flow of prana there.

9- Release all bandhas and quickly inhale, letting the bliss rush upward through Sushumna Nadi until it ecstatically explodes in the Crown Chakra (Sahasrara). Roll your eyes upward toward the Crown Chakra, comfortably performing Shambhavi Mudra as you inhale. The Kundalini energy may activate because of this.

Repeat this practice multiple times (at least for 12 rounds or 20 minutes; you can use a japamala to keep count). The more you do it, the greater the chance that you will manage to raise strong pranic currents and awaken the inner fire, which will fill your subtle body with intense bliss and emptiness. If you're a beginner, start by practicing only six rounds or ten minutes, and gradually build up the number of rounds. Take things slowly. Remember that the preliminary practices are important to still the body and mind first, and to get them into a state more prone to performing this practice successfully. Of course, you can perform this method as a stand-alone if you so desire, but it won't have the same potency.

Because you're not holding the breath for as long on the inhalation like with Kriya Supreme Fire, it will have way fewer adverse side effects. However, you can still experience some uncomfortable after-effects such as impatience, headaches, insomnia, or energy overload. How many of these

116

you experience always depends on your level of ripeness and spiritual maturity. To counteract this, I give my usual advice: interact with nature; walk barefoot on a beach; connect with animals, trees, and plants; swim in the sea; or just self-pace accordingly. Performing asanas or doing some form of physical exercise will also help tremendously to regulate the energy and potential side effects. It's also one of the most fun and beneficial grounding exercises you can do because it will improve your overall health, from muscles to bones to the cardiovascular and pulmonary system, etc. And don't forget to get enough sleep.

If you're just starting, it is best to let the body slowly get used to the new levels of energy that will be generated by pacing yourself and going gently with the practice. Don't attempt to do too much at the same time.

Due to the tremendous power this practice generates, it will dissolve stubborn blockages in your subtle body and unlock a lot of unconscious pollution that you might have accumulated throughout this life (or others), including deep-rooted fears and subtle feelings concealed beneath rational thought. These can be painful to experience but surfacing unconscious debris in the psyche in order to be purified is part of a seeker's spiritual progress. Conversely, there will also be many incredibly blissful experiences to compensate.

Sometimes, an intense bliss and heat may inundate you so strongly that you temporarily dissolve into an all-encompassing unity. However, it is also completely possible to just lose consciousness and forget what happened. If you become unconscious, as soon as you "come back," just keep doing what you were doing. Remember not to force anything; things should be gentle, subtle, and naturally blissful. Here, losing consciousness is not synonymous with fainting—it's just that your conscious mind is still limited and unable to remain conscious in deeper levels of being.

Tantric Fire prompts the awakening of the vast reservoir of life-force laying in potential in the Muladhara, which rises toward the higher centers through Sushumna Nadi, passing through all the chakras, culminating in the supremely bliss-fully experience of wholeness in Sahasrara[20]. Typically, the life-force doesn't flow within Sushumna Nadi but through the subtle side channels, *Ida* and *Pingala*, located on either side of the spinal column. Humans spend their lives swinging between both of these channels, which symbolize duality. When prana goes through the central canal, it's always for

---

[20] This pranic energy that rises through Sushumna Nadi is called *Udana Vayu*, the "ascending air" or "vertical breath." Once it reaches the Crown Chakra, it is transformed into *Vyana Vayu*, the "omnipresent" or "all-pervading" air. Normally, this air pervades the whole body, but following the course and transformations mentioned above, it permeates the whole universe rather than just an individual body.

spiritual purposes. Therefore, via Sushumna Nadi, we're always going directly toward unity.

> "The medial nadi is located in the middle [Sushumna Nadi]. It is as slender as the stem of a lotus. If one meditates on the inner vacuity of this nadi, in the form of the Shakti [Kundalini], then the Divine [Shiva; pure consciousness] is revealed."
>
> - VIJÑĀNA-BHAIRAVA-TANTRA

When the practice ends, just stay silent, being present. Let your body and mind dwell and integrate everything that's going on within you. After a great deal of consistent and well-performed practice, you will begin to experience a blissful emptiness in this after-state, which pervades your body and mind, and you may also feel a burst of rapture at the center of the heart chakra. If you just stay like that, being engulfed by the blissful emptiness, you will effortlessly "enter" into a Self-Awareness state that is not like your typical day-to-day awareness. It's more like a blissful heightened awareness of "just being." You're simply conscious of being. Consciousness becomes conscious of itself.

When this happens, stay as long as you can in this state. This state is the most sacred portal toward Self-Realization.

It is a prelude to the enlightenment beingness state—a natural, effortless, empty nondual bliss awareness. If this "state" happens, not at the end, but during the practice, or at any moment of the day, let go of everything and melt in it! It's such a blessing, and when it naturally starts happening more and more, you know you are unlocking a huge door toward freedom.

That being said, if your unconscious tendencies and mental impressions are still strong enough to pull your attention out of such Self-Consciousness "state," and prevent you from experiencing the disappearance of your "I-ego," you just need to continue practicing, returning over and over to the practice until you dissolve these samskaras and karmic anchors. Once you overcome a certain threshold, there will be no need to keep purifying or cleaning blockages anymore because the Self-Consciousness "state" will automatically do everything required to (*Tan*) expand the recognition of its own immortal consciousness, thereby (*tra*) saving the ignorant individual consciousness from the illusion of being a separate entity. This is the real discovery of the experiential meaning of the word Tantra—it becomes your living reality.

CHAPTER 11

THE FIRE AND THE EMBERS

Many aspirants believe that Tantra has the sole purpose of integrating sexuality and instincts into a meditative and spiritual path. But this is not so, as we've seen throughout this volume. As you progress on your spiritual path, sexuality becomes a natural and integrated part of your life, regardless of how you express it.

Instead of compressing sexual energy into the first two chakras and then discharging the excess energy, which gives a false sense of relief from the confines of the self, you can uplift that excess energy.

However, in humans, sexuality is seldom integrated as a normal part of life. It is often seen that a person has either repressed/hidden their sexuality or has become controlled and consumed by it. Extremes are never good, and as an aspirant progresses on their spiritual path, they will eventually

121

contemplate and learn how to integrate their instincts. This is a natural integration, although one may have their doubts, having seen many supposedly enlightened gurus fall prey to their own instincts, traumatizing many seekers in the process.

Albeit poorly understood, you should know that you don't need to perform "tantric sex" to sublimate your sexual energy for spiritual use. Many spiritual practices do that already, just as the ones shared in this book do.

There is a very famous quote in *Vijñāna-bhairava-tantra* which says:

> "At the start of sexual union,
> keep attention on the fire in the beginning,
> and, so continuing, avoid the embers in the end."

This quote has been used as the muse for a multitude of books authored by many famous gurus. It essentially implies that sexual union should not end with an "actual" orgasm, but should instead be prolonged as much as possible to cultivate and harness sexual energy in order to elevate it toward the higher subtle centers while the mind sinks into its source of blissful consciousness. This has the purpose of generating a higher state which can then be used for Self-Realization. In other words, it proposes that neither man nor woman should sexually climax but rather surf the wave of bliss, redirecting it toward the awakening of the Kundalini to experience the loss of self and become enlightened.

It is true that the bliss achieved through the sexual act can be used as a means for Self-Realization if continuously maintained and properly redirected (we've already learned how to use any type of bliss as our practice's main focal point). However, as we've previously addressed in this book, the vast majority of seekers will not be able to do this successfully, and it can easily become misused or may even transform into a blockage. When this happens, it can lead to self-justified indulgence, which is always rationalized by the mind as being for "spiritual reasons."

Nonetheless, since Tantra always attempts to integrate all types of practices, it is up to you, if you so desire, to perform tantric fire practices in any situation where bliss is present. I leave that to your discretion.

Just keep in mind the following:

If any guru implies that you should practice "tantric sex" to awaken Sushumna Nadi, raise the Kundalini, and explore the unconscious to get enlightened, then it is my opinion that you should stay away from them. In the end, most of the time, things will not end well for you.

There are better ways to achieve these results, as I've shared in my books and teachings. If you're eagerly looking into Tantra as a way to use your sensual pleasures for spiritual liberation, because some ancient scripture or guru said it's possible, you should look again. What's really the reason? This is something you should meditate on. The ego is very tricky, and it tries to appropriate everything it can, including spiritual subjects.

Here's what a spiritual seeker wants:

"I want to let go of suffering, transcend my own limitations, and attain the nondual plenitude of blissful being, feeling utterly realized."

However, here's what the ego wants:

"I don't really want enlightenment because I want to stay as I currently am; My existence depends on the continuity of illusion and ignorance.

However, if I have no choice but to enroll in a spiritual path, and my only two options to achieve enlightenment are:

1- Sitting meditative practices, purifying my unconscious tendencies, mental impressions, subconscious patterns, doing energy work, being lucid throughout the day, looking at the "I," being conscious of consciousness, studying proper spiritual teachings, and surrendering to God.

Versus

2- Embracing sensual pleasures, luxuriating into instincts, and practicing "transgressive" Tantra.

I will unquestionably choose the second!"

When the ego is presented with such a decision, it will always try to sabotage itself through whatever means, always self-justifying each choice through rationalization. That's why such an approach can be extremely irresponsible and imprudent. Nonetheless, at the end of the day, it is up to each one of us to decide how we want to cross the spiritual path. We can try many things and then decide what is the best way to achieve our goal. No two persons are the same, and no two paths are the same.

That being said, this doesn't mean that you cannot sublimate your own instincts and sensual desires in order to use them as the means for spiritual advancement.

DESIRE TRANSMUTATION

There are methods that can be used to redirect instinctual forces into spiritual desire and motivation.

There are two instinctive forces in the body-mind that are above all others: the *libido*, which is a force related to the reproduction of the species (i.e., sexual drive); and *self-preservation*, which is the force related to the survival of the species (i.e., the survival instinct). They are both interconnected and have a primal role in the functioning of living beings.

Through spiritual practice, including the practices of Tantric Fire and Mula Bandha as shared in this book, these two instinctual energies can be harvested and transformed into a higher energy with spiritual aims, instead of being completely spent on ephemeral phenomena and mental soap operas. They can also be converted into a super intense desire for Self-Realization. This super intense desire is unlike all other desires because it will burn them all, like a burning log that consumes all the other logs when placed together. This yearning is the main factor that will determine whether or not you will become liberated. Yes, the intensity of your desire is that important—and without it, you will not go far. It is what distinguishes real aspirants from wannabe seekers.

Once aspirants realize that all of the "common" blisses they experience are just the tip of the iceberg compared to the ecstasy that can be experienced through Tantric practice, they will want to take up the spiritual path and bathe directly in the unending divine bliss that is their birthright. Divine bliss that is experienced in the higher subtle centers feels less "human" or sexual in nature, and more "otherworldly," "exotic," or, as the name suggests, "divine," always expanding toward an all-encompassing Oneness.

When this happens, the orgasmic pleasure derived from sexual activity (i.e., from the lower chakras) will no longer seem as important or attractive to you. A sure sign that your energy is dwelling in the higher centers rather than the lower is that now you yearn only for the endless fountain of bliss that your original Being is made of. You have redirected the instinctive forces in your psyche to a higher purpose—the eternal repose in God's lap.

Part 3

THE IMMANENCE OF TRANSCENDENCE

Everything is One: A single reality consisting of Consciousness alone, pure and blissful, unbroken by time, uncircumscribed by space, unclouded by attributes, unconfined by appearances, unexpressed by words, beyond all ordinary means of knowledge.

- ABHINAVAGUPTA,
TANTRASARA

CHAPTER 12

SHIVA CONSCIOUSNESS

"Awareness is the sole cause of Liberation."

- ABHINAVAGUPTA,

TANTRALOKA

At the beginning of this volume, the meaning of the word Tantra was brought to light:

Tan = continuation, to expand.

Tra = instrument of, save, protection.

Tantra allows the seeker *to expand* their individual consciousness into the universal domain of consciousness and *save* themselves from ignorance/*protect* themselves from the illusory Maya. It is an *instrument of* liberation by providing us with a way to tap into the transpersonal field and realize the unbroken *continuation* of Absolute Consciousness, which is

131

another name for Shiva Consciousness. Establishing yourself in Shiva Consciousness is what enlightenment is all about.

After performing and progressing in spiritual practice, contemplating the teachings, and adopting a more tantric or spiritual worldview and lifestyle, there comes a time, sooner or later (always depending on how quickly you progress and integrate the teachings, insights, and states), where you have to turn your attention to the presence of Being itself. This means that the very same subject of practice must turn itself into its own "object" of attention.

By continuously subjecting the subject to its own self-attentive state, Tantra acquires a purely nondual format. There is no energy, chakras, or mental concept that the subject (you) can use as support because emptiness has permeated and collapsed them all. You don't need to view anyone or even yourself as pure consciousness either, as that would imply imagination, a struggle, and a belief. What you need is to recognize and establish yourself in yourself through your own direct experience. You will be merging your foreground of experience into your background of awareness, immersing your individual consciousness into universal consciousness.

You can achieve this by paying attention to your own sense of "I," allowing it to be absorbed by its transpersonal source. Focus on the "I-ness," "I am," or on the source of "I." There's no struggle, tension, reaching out, attaining, or accomplishing when one abides in the subjective dimension. It's more of a "resting into awareness" than using effort; it's a surrender of your personhood into godhood. It is just being still with your whole being, "just being," while remaining aware. There is no distinction between the goal and the path here because the path itself—consciousness blissfully aware of itself—is the goal.

Fundamentally, this method involves bringing your attention out of its ordinary abode in external or internal objects, and shifting it to the very source of attention itself. It's redirecting one of the most critical facets of the dynamic consciousness (attention) into the unmoving substratum that powers it. This redirecting of attention into itself will result in great insights, bliss, and a feeling of insurmountable peace. It brings about the realization of our true nature.

Truth be told, this is the most refined method to realize your true nature, and although it may seem "hard" to do, it's only a lack of discernment that gives rise to such a thought. In fact, you are already aware, and you don't need to do anything else other than paying attention to that fact. However, if you are still constantly bombarded by thoughts and restlessness, if your ability to relax and concentrate is still subpar, or if your pranic energy is still predisposed to staying in the lower chakras, then this practice will be impossible to do correctly because the subtle mental noise is just too pronounced and distracting. If this is the case, you still need to do more work on the previous practices.

There may also be times when you'll switch from nondual sadhana back to subject-object practices, and it's perfectly fine to do so. On some days, subtle thoughts, concepts, or mental constructs will seem to linger in the periphery of your mind longer than usual, and you just can't ignore or let them go. Hence, instead of forcing nondual practice that seems to go nowhere, you go back to the object-based practices for a while.

Nonetheless, this intuitive "knowingness" of being aware is just that—being conscious of being conscious; noticing the fact that you are aware. Recognizing subjective attention (i.e., attention to the subject instead of the object) is entering and establishing oneself into the realm of Shiva. By staying within this realm of experienceless experience, free from thoughts, sensations, images, or perceptions, you make pure consciousness your abode.

When practiced regularly with a spiritually mature mind, this will strip off all of the subtle remaining conditioning and propel you to integrate your natural state of Being into your dual form. But before you're able to make this "stateless state" permanent, it'll appear to come and go. It's as if you were brought "into" it and then unwillingly lose it.

This natural state doesn't come and go, but it may seem like it, just like silence seems to come and go, yet it's the ever-present substratum of noise. To overcome this, the continuity of nondual practice (attention to one's own consciousness) is a constant requirement.

To discover its ever-present nature, you need to allow it to be by nonchalantly bathing in and surrendering into it so that its presence becomes easily recognizable even amid dual states and mental subtleties.

This nondual practice is relatively easy to perform, yet it continues to elude many. Most of the time, this occurs because practitioners are underprepared—their mind is just too immature, restless, and lacks the proper insight and depth to perform it correctly. They have failed to find their "I am-ness" and dwell in it. Moreover, many aspirants still disregard nondual practice and focus on dualistic techniques.

Usually, they think that such nondual sadhana is too abstract from a practical standpoint. They prefer the complex technical and mechanical processes of a dualistic spiritual practice. This doesn't come as a surprise, and it shows a lack of discernment and maturity. In its quest for self-survival, the ego will always prefer to perform practices based on the mind and its movements rather than something that would illuminate and collapse the "I" itself.

However, being conscious of consciousness is much more "potent" than what the mind would have you believe. Although it might start off as an "I" actively focusing upon itself and seem like a "doing," it will eventually stop being an "I" inside a spacious impersonal Presence, and will evolve into an impersonal Presence-Beingness being itself. This is the transition from duality to nonduality—a going from "trying to just be," "trying to be conscious of consciousness," or "trying to do nothing" to actually "just being," "conscious of consciousness," and "doing nothing," respectively. As you keep on practicing, you will become ever more established in Shiva Consciousness, though it is never absent, until nonduality becomes your permanent home from which you've never left.

But this isn't the end because Tantra integrates nonduality within duality: it leads Shakti into Shiva[21] and then brings Shiva into Shakti, coming full circle and dissolving all distinctions. Body, mind, energy, and spirit are all integrated through the tantric path, and such a being becomes the living embodiment of God, uniting the personal with the impersonal—nonduality becomes personal, and duality becomes universal. This is the Unfathomable experiencing life.

---

[21] It should be understood, though, that Shakti is not "outside" of Shiva. Shakti emerges out of Shiva without ever leaving Shiva, as there's nothing outside of pure consciousness.

CHAPTER 13

THE TANTRIKA

The vast majority of spiritual traditions shun both our individuality and the manifest world, only addressing the nondual and transcendental aspects of spirituality. The separation of nondual and dual, manifest and unmanifest, and transcendental and ordinary is something that prevents full integration of the realization of pure consciousness.

Tantra doesn't shun duality or individuality; it actually embraces them. It goes beyond transcendence because it doesn't exclude what it transcends, but rather integrates.

Tantra brings the realization of Oneness and the realization of Multipleness, by allowing us to see difference in unity and unity in difference. Without neglecting phenomena or their essence, Tantra makes the connection between the light of our consciousness and its reflection as phenomena. It allows us to manifest nonduality in the dual world of name and form, and bring our dual form into the melting oven of unmanifested Oneness.

We can discover our unbounded nature through a state of expansion—we expand beyond the boundaries of our current limited consciousness into the universal dimension of consciousness. But we can also rediscover our boundary-lessness by piercing the surface of a state of contraction. This contracted state is not a damnation, but rather an opportunity to discover and experience God's infiniteness.

This world and the experiences it provides can and should be enjoyed through our dualistic form. I'd go so far as to say that the true enjoyment of duality only begins after we have liberated ourselves from the illusion of being the enjoyer. A free being is free to experience life's true colors—its highs and lows. After all, Tantra guides you toward freedom *in the world*, not from it.

Every perception, every feeling, every emotion, every action, and every moment are like a beautiful line of a painting pregnant with the colorless signature of consciousness.

Some spiritual schools vehemently point out the unreality of the world. Yes, the world is unreal, just like an illusion is. An illusion is a misinterpreted perception or a deceptive appearance or impression; it's something that is not what it seems to be. It's the classic story of mistaking a rope for a snake. With sufficient light, we realize that what was once thought to be a snake is actually just a rope. However, it is often seen that many practitioners of such schools use an escapist view of "world = bad" as a way of avoiding facing their own issues and as an attempt to bypass the uneasiness that comes with sensory deprivation. Such a dissociative view—usually accompanied by a firm conviction of the meaninglessness of everything due to the knowledge of the impermanent nature of all things—goes, in essence, against the core principles of Tantra. Often, a denial-based "life is suffering" type of path typically ends in the void of nihilism.

Tantra does embrace the void of selflessness, but then overcomes it by finding the bliss of Being, which is transpersonal, and brings such lightless light into the dual realm of the world. The tantric path doesn't end in self-denial but in self-love. Instead of taking us only toward transcendental divinity, Tantra lets us know that the realization of divinity right here, right now—the immanence of the divine—is also part of the metaphysical equation. But to grasp this insight in its full practical dimension, you must first awaken to your nondual nature, as explained in the previous chapter.

If you are a follower of Tantra, you can be said to be a tantrika. But those who have discovered their true nature are no ordinary tantrikas—they are adept tantrikas. They have used Tantra in its intended meaning, as an instrument for the expansion of consciousness.

Now, this insight must be aligned at all levels, including in the experience of body and duality, until there's an undifferentiated continuum of perception. This means that despite being able to discern objects, no boundaries are created in relation to their essence. One is like a goldsmith who, rather than merely seeing all of the different forms of jewelry, is perfectly capable of seeing them all as only gold. This doesn't imply that everything is considered to be the same. There's still diversity, but it may sound like a paradox to a mind that only works logically. The goldsmith can appreciate the various forms of gold jewelry and can even create beautiful pieces, but he can also see them all as what they really are: gold.

This is what distinguishes a tantrika: instead of negating duality in favor of nonduality, the tantrika transcends transcendence to find immanence. They find nonduality within duality.

CHAPTER 14

TANTRIC SURRENDER

On the tantric path, even after realizing who you truly are, in order to come full circle, you have to bring forth the knowledge of your realization and embody it into your vehicle of dualistic existence—the body.

Just because you have experientially realized that you are, in essence, pure consciousness—through the constant abiding in empty blissful consciousness—that doesn't mean that the "density" and "solidity" of your feeling of having a body will simply disappear. It may, but it most likely won't. It's like the smoke of an already extinguished fire. Not everyone will experience the body and perceive the world in a way that is coherent with the direct insight or understanding of their true nature; there may be a divergence between what you know you are (because you have experienced it directly) and how you perceive and feel in your dualistic existence.

Take the example of someone who went through an amputation and experiences phantom limb pain. Although their limb is no longer there, they experience sensations/pain as if they still had it. It's a residual feeling, and due to subconscious habit, the brain continues sending these signals as if nothing has changed. A similar thing can occur with Self-Realization; just because you realize that you are not the body—you are bodiless consciousness—that doesn't mean that your experience of the body will go in line with your current understanding and realization. Typically, the body, because it's a "grosser dimension," will take longer to be permeated by such insight.

Through this tantric practice, you will align this understanding. And don't worry, it's not like you will go crazy and won't be able to distinguish between where the physical body ends and where something else begins. What occurs is that duality becomes interconnected as a unified field of experience: you bring unity into diversity, experiencing duality through the nondual lens. The sensations of the body don't have to disappear; you just experience them differently, as another modulation of consciousness. It's similar to the goldsmith example from the previous chapter.

To overcome the current limiting experience of the body, you will take a raw look at what the body ("me") and the world ("not me/otherness") actually are. You will discern their unseparateness and permeate them with the bliss and peace inherent to consciousness. The entire dimension of the dualistic experience in this world must be infused with the fragrance of blissful consciousness.

Unlike in Tantra, this isn't directly addressed in most nondual spiritual traditions. The reason this occurs is because you can indirectly achieve a similar outcome through gradually bathing and melting in consciousness as consciousness, over and over again. In Tantra, however, you can directly and actively begin dissolving those residual impressions and sensations as soon as you acquire proper maturity in being able to stay as empty consciousness through nondual sadhana.

First, you distance yourself from all objective experiences, including the dense feeling of the body and worldly perceptions, and contemplate your true boundless nature. "I am not that which I can be aware of, but that which is aware" is the insight. You are capable of witnessing, from an unmoving and untouchable place, that everything is a temporary appearance that comes and goes. But you, as consciousness, are not fleeting; you are like a transparent, empty, eternal, and unlocalizable "presence of Being."

Having realized that your true nature is blissful bodiless consciousness, you now return to the objects and perceptions in order to dismantle their apparent separation because there may be remnants of an opaque, condensed, bounded, and localizable nature—the body. You want to dissolve this smoke once and for all, infusing the light of your discovery into your own body. Tantric teachings are heavy proponents of the view that if the realization is not settled in all of our dimensions, including how we perceive the body and the world, then it's still incomplete.

When you contemplate the experience of your body, what do you experience?

Try it right now. Close your eyes and feel what the experience of having a body is made of; allow it to come into your field of attention. Not a thought, memory, or image about the body, but the actual experience of the body. Don't conceptualize or think about the body; just sense the raw experience of having a body.

Did you notice what the experience of having a body consists of? It's just sensations. The experience of the body is made of sensations, a flow of sensations arising in the space of consciousness. This shouldn't be news because we've already tackled the feeling of body identification in the first part of this book.

Now, imagine a vase. The vase (body) gives the illusion that the space inside of it (limited consciousness) is separate from the space outside of it (infinite consciousness). But in fact, the vase is within the all-encompassing space that is outside of itself. The space within the vase (limited consciousness) is no different than the space outside of the vase (all-pervading consciousness), but it seems so because of the vase's walls.

The idea that the vase separates the space within it from the outside is just an illusion. If the space within the vase were to investigate such an assumption, it would discover the truth: the experience of being inside the vase (body) is just a sensation, and it can be transformed into an experience of being everywhere (all-pervading space), with the vase within it, instead of being limited by the vase. The space inside the vase now knows itself to be the whole space; it just so happens that there's a vase within it. Consciousness is just like space. And even the apparent "solidity" of the vase itself is not as straightforward as it may appear.

"For the power of space is inherent in the individual soul as the true subjectivity, which is at once empty of objects and which also provides a place in which objects may be known."

- ABHINAVAGUPTA,
PARATRISIKA-LAGHUVRTTI

Keep noticing the direct experience of the body, regardless of whether you have your eyes opened or closed. Again, don't think or imagine; just feel the raw sensations of having a body. Some sensations are very subtle, almost unnoticeable, while others are more vivid and intense. You may feel a tingling sensation all over the body (or you might notice more of this as you focus on a specific part), the sensations of the feet touching the ground, or just dormancy in some regions. If some part of your body hurts, you will feel that sensation and you will notice that it's a bit more intense than other sensations. If you've been reading or looking at a screen for a while, you might experience a slight weight or "burning" sensation in your eyes. You may also feel hunger, which is a sensation as well.

These are all sensations that you associate with the body. When you feel that you have a body, it's all of these sensations agglomerated that give rise to the feeling of having a body. Notice that, for example, hearing a sound or seeing something with your eyes is not an experience of the body but an experience of the world. In this practice, we're primarily focused on the experience of the body.

Continue delving into and exploring your body's sensations as they pulsate and vibrate, and infuse them with the bliss and emptiness inherent to pure consciousness. Do this by focusing on these sensations and then bringing forth the blissful "state" of empty consciousness. You are exchanging your limited experience of the body as these sensations, into the unlimited "experience" of the bliss and emptiness of consciousness. You are capable of doing this because, now, you can "tap" into the signature of blissful consciousness and bring its perfume into the experience of the body. Instead of stopping at the objectivity of the body or sense experiences, you penetrate their core and bring their inner signature of consciousness to light.

In other words, you are permeating the vase itself with space until it gets transparent enough that, even though it is there, there's no separation between the space inside the vase and that outside of it.

You've already had the experience and insight of being the whole space (both inside and outside). Now, through this tantric practice of melting sensations and boundaries, you are surrendering your experience of the body in order to get it aligned with your understanding and realization of your true boundless nature as pure consciousness. After all, you want your day-to-day dual experience of life to be consistent with your realization.

Do not try to move energy, manipulate sensations, or change anything. Just feel the raw, unadulterated sensations and then permeate them with luminous awareness, progressively dissolving these superimposed feelings within the space of consciousness. These sensations are not solid; they're just energetic vibrations and tingling. Through this practice, you will notice that they are just modulations of the same awareness that is aware of them, thereby dissolving their apparent independent existence as a limited feeling of a body. As you keep doing this, you begin to experience the quintessence of the body, revealing its underlying nature, experientially, as blissful consciousness.

Ultimately, there is no difference between the experience of the body and unbounded consciousness. The feeling of the body, which initially seems like a collection of sensations arising in the space of consciousness, is like a stream of water in a vast, still ocean. It is moving and seems to be a limited "thing" ("a stream") while consciousness seems calm and unlimited ("the still ocean"), but they're really the same— they're both water. The stream of water doesn't have to stop being a current—it just has to lose its feeling of bodily separation and be the whole ocean, which includes the current. After all, the current is not an independent "thing" but is simply moving water. Similarly, there's no such thing as an individual and independently existing "body"—it's just a vibration of consciousness, a "pulsation" of awareness.

As long as you have the inner knowingness or insight of your true nature as pure consciousness, *and* are able to abide in it as it (empty presence of consciousness), then you can embark on this practice of exploring and enlightening the experience of the body and of everything related to it. It's also essential to return to it over and over again, gradually washing away the old residual feelings of the experience of the body.

"Shankara (...) made three statements:
Brahman [consciousness] is real.
The Universe is unreal.
Brahman is the Universe."

- THE TEACHINGS OF RAMANA MAHARSHI
EDITED BY ARTHUR OSBORNE

Brahman is pure consciousness. It is real. The universe of names and forms (Maya) is unreal. But if we penetrate the illusion of Maya, we discover that the universe of names and forms is actually made of pure consciousness!

The same applies to our experience of the body: pure consciousness is real; the body is unreal; pure consciousness is actually the body!

149

You've gone from believing that you were the body (consciousness has acquired the name, form, and limitations of the body) to realize that you are unbounded consciousness (consciousness rediscovers its limitless nature). But now you go even further and recognize that the body is actually unbounded consciousness (the body stands revealed as consciousness itself)!

The bodily sensations don't proclaim "I am a separate, independent entity" anymore, and "I am everything" roars freely in a unified field of experience. Without boundaries, everything is one! It has never not been like this; you just didn't recognize it before.

This is tantric surrender—the sacrificial offer of the body to God.

CHAPTER 15

THE KNIFE GRINDER

When I was little, I met a street knife grinder. He was a reserved person and rarely uttered a word. When I first saw his knife sharpening machinery, I noticed that it had pedals—it looked like a really strange mini-bicycle.

He was using a pedal-powered grinding machine that moved an abrasive wheel, which was used to sharpen the knives.

With his face wrinkled from the sun beating down on the stairway of time, and his eyes steadily fixed on the knife, he became a modern-day alchemist: he transformed a blunt tool into a razor-sharp instrument of cutting.

As he was sharpening the knives, he kept grinding them against the hard, rough surface of the abrasive wheel.

One day, I brought him an old knife to see it get sharpened. As he was griding it, I noticed that he poured water onto the wheel, and I got curious: "Why the water?" I asked.

He looked at me, cracked a small smile, and stated: "Grinding the knife like this generates heat and also dries out the wheel. I put water to make it less dry and to lower its heat so that I don't accidentally burn my hand or arm."

I thanked him for the explanation. Once he finished, he gave me back the knife, and now it was even sharper than when I had first bought it. Strangely enough, that was the last day I ever saw him.

Now, many years later, I had forgotten about the whole thing until I suddenly remembered it while writing this book. Why would I remember such a thing, and does it have to do with Tantra?

Well, this is exactly like Tantra.

Your mind is the knife; it is not sharp enough at the moment to properly cut anything hard. Because your consciousness thinks it's the body (giving rise to what we call "I-ego" and mind"), it is too blunt to cut through its limitations. However, the system of Tantra (the wheel) makes your mind (the knife) sharp enough to cut through the illusion of Maya. When the knife is going through the grinding process (while your mind is being purified through sadhana), it generates heat (inner fire, Kundalini energy). Sometimes water (grounding) is necessary to calm the energy down and prevent it from overheating.

The pedals of the machinery are what power the wheel (Tantra). This book represents the pedals—it can power Tantra because it gives you the tools that enable you to use the wheel and sharpen your ability to cut through the ignorance and the illusion of being a limited time-bound separate entity that experiences misery and suffering.

You are the knife grinder. It's up to you to turn the pedals and get the whole system going.

Of course, the tantric path isn't smooth, but no genuine spiritual path is. You'll be grinding your limited conscious-ness against the hard, rough surface of self-investigation and self-contemplation through tantric practice, via abrasion—you'll be scraping away the "limited" part of consciousness in order to reveal its limitlessness.

Encountering the reality of your individual disintegration, the end of your identity as you know it—the grand finale of your conceptual self—and embodying such transpersonal perfume seems like an intimidating and arduous endeavor. Maybe it is. But to achieve anything worthwhile, motivation, perseverance, and hard work are always requirements, regardless of whether we're talking about spirituality or not.

Struggles and downfalls will always happen, and life will test you. But as you travel down the path, you will discover that the roughness of the road ahead is insignificant because you'll learn how to fly.

And you know what? The yearning to fly is profoundly ingrained in the human spirit; it is the longing for freedom. This is what Tantra is all about: showing you your wings. Now fly and be free!

If you've enjoyed reading this book and feel that it has made a positive difference in the way you see and approach the art of Tantra, please show your support by leaving a *Review on the Amazon page.*

It really makes a difference. It helps to spread genuine spiritual teachings to those who are truly seeking them.

Thank you for reading.

Subscribe and receive the eBook **Uncovering the Real** plus updates and information regarding new books or articles, which will be sent about once or twice a month.

www.RealYoga.info

If you have any doubts or questions regarding this or any of the other books, feel free to contact me at:

Santata@RealYoga.info

Read also, by the same author of this book:

— KRIYA YOGA EXPOSED *[REAL YOGA BOOK #1]*

This is not your common guide to Kriya Yoga. It is something you've never seen before. This book brings to light the truth about the current Kriya Yoga Gurus & Organizations. It also contains the explanation of Kriya Yoga techniques, including the Final Special Kriya.

— THE SECRET POWER OF KRIYA YOGA *[REAL YOGA BOOK #2]*

Revealing the fastest Path to Enlightenment. Learn how to fuse Bhakti and Jnana Yoga into Kriya Yoga to unleash the most powerful Yoga ever. After exposing Kriya Yoga in the first volume of this collection, we will now unleash its tremendous power as the basis for all Yogas to come into fruition, going beyond our apparent existence and mortality, into the realmless realms of the Absolute beyond comprehension.

— KUNDALINI EXPOSED *[REAL YOGA BOOK #3]*

Kundalini has been one of the most mysterious and well-kept secrets in the history of spirituality. Not anymore. The book that discloses the Cosmic mystery of Kundalini. The Ultimate Guide to Kundalini Yoga, Kundalini Awakening, Rising, and Reposing on its Hidden Throne.

— THE YOGA OF CONSCIOUSNESS *[REAL YOGA BOOK #4]*

This book contains 25 Direct Practices to Enlightenment. It unveils the ultimate practical guide to Non-Duality (Advaita) and uncovers the unseen blockages made by the ego-mind, in a profound yet accessible way. It goes beyond Spirituality into Awakening Non-Duality.

— TURIYA: THE GOD STATE *[REAL YOGA BOOK #5]*

Unravel the ancient mystery of Turiya - The God State. The book that demystifies and uncovers the true state of Enlightened beings. The teachings and expositions in this book are unlike anything you've ever seen. Special paragraphs were written with the underlying purpose of dismantling the illusory constructs that your ego-mind has created.

— SAMADHI: THE FORGOTTEN EDEN *[SERENADE OF BLISS BOOK #1]*

Revealing the Ancient Yogic Art of Samadhi. This book unveils the ancient art of how yogis and mystics had the keys to an unlimited reservoir of wisdom and power. It brings the timeless and forgotten wisdom of Samadhi into modern-day practicality.

— THE YOGIC DHARMA *[SERENADE OF BLISS BOOK #2]*

Revealing the underlying essence of the Yamas and Niyamas. A profound and unconventional exposition on the spirit of the Yogic Dharma principles. Although they've been distorted to fit today's "self-help chocolate" culture, this book will change that—it will turn your world upside down.

— LUCID DREAMING: THE PATH OF NON-DUAL DREAM YOGA

[SERENADE OF BLISS BOOK #3]

Lucid dreaming like you've never seen before. Can you realize your true nature through Lucid Dreaming? Most seekers would say no. But this work is not a common lucid dreaming book—it elevates the ancient art of lucid dreaming into non-dual Dream Yoga to realize your true nature (enlightenment).

All of these books are available @ Amazon as Kindle & Paperback.

GLOSSARY

Advaita – Nonduality.

Asana – Body posture; a sitting pose for spiritual practice.

Background of Consciousness / Awareness – Another name for pure Awareness. However, such a name presupposes that there is a foreground or that which is witnessed, implying a duality. That's quite right, but it should be understood that this name is a helpful clue for seekers because it helps them take a step back from the mental contents with which they are usually identified, so that they can repose in awareness itself.

Beingness – The intrinsic nature of consciousness is "Being." To be is to be conscious. At first, "Beingness" might be felt as a profound experience of stillness, peace, joy, etc., but as one goes further, it will dissolve our individuality, and our blissful Oneness will shine through.

Chakra – Wheel/plexus, a psychic-energy center.

Ego – "I," the thought "I" or "I-ego." It is the erroneous belief of being a separate being or entity. For a more in-depth understanding, refer to *The Yoga of Consciousness*.

Energy Body – The **subtle body** (*Suksma sarira*) is the body between the causal body (*Anandamaya kosha*) and the physical body (*Sthula sarira* or *Annamaya kosha*). According to Vedantic philosophy, it is composed of three "sheaths": the "energy sheath" (the energy body, *pranamaya kosha; prana or life-force*), the "mind sheath" (*manomaya kosha; the mind*), and the "intellect sheath" (*Vijnanmaya kosha; the intellect or the ability to discriminate*).

159

Enlightenment – The realization of your true nature/original state of unbounded happiness and peace; Self-realization; Nirvana; Mukti; Refer to the *Real Yoga Series* for a comprehensive explanation.

God – God is neither male nor female. God is not a person or an entity—that would make God limited. God is the all-pervading Consciousness, being formless, timeless, and unborn. It is the infinite Awareness that each one of us possesses, and out of which everything is "made."

Ida Nadi – The left subtle channel.

Ishta-Devata – Personal God; the form one attributes to the formless Consciousness.

Japamala – A string of prayer beads commonly used in spiritual practices.

Jiva – Individual self.

Kundalini – The primal spiritual energy said to be located at the base of the spine. Cosmic Kundalini is the same energy but rather than being the individual's latent energy, it is the universal latent energy, being infinitely more powerful.

Mantra – Sacred syllable or word or set of words.

Maya – The veil of illusion that appears to cover our true infinite nature. This veil allows pure empty consciousness to believe it has divided itself into many different forms, each with different qualities, from beings to thoughts to galaxies. It is the **manifested relative**: the contents of Awareness that have manifested from its infinite potential.

Neo-Tantra – The modern, westernized, and sexualized variation of Tantra.

Nonduality or **Nondual state** – "Not two;" i.e., a stateless state where only consciousness blissfully aware of itself exists; the end of the dichotomy of "I" and "other." The original natural state of being. Nonduality cannot be truly described in a glossary; refer to *Turiya – The God State*.

Pingala Nadi – The right subtle channel.

Prana – Life-force.

Pranayama – Life-force restraint/control technique.

Pure Consciousness – Our pure and true formless Self-aware nature. That which is conscious; Is your body conscious? No. Is your brain conscious? No. We could go on all day until we realize that nothing is conscious by itself, except consciousness. I use Consciousness and Awareness interchangeably throughout this book.

Sadhana – Spiritual Practice.

Self – With a capital "S" means pure consciousness or pure Awareness, devoid of any objects; self with a small "s" is synonymous with ego or "I."

Shakti – Personification of Kundalini, the life-force principle that gives life to the Universe.

Shaktipat – An energetic transmission given by the Guru to the disciple; the descent of "divine grace;" a shift in the consciousness of the seeker.

Shiva – Personification of the Absolute Consciousness. For some, he is the Hindu God who is the destroyer of the Universe.

Subconscious mind – That which is beneath the conscious mind. Sometimes, it is also called the "unconscious."

Sushumna Nadi – The subtle channel through which the life-force flows, located in the middle of the spinal cord.

Vasanas / Samskaras – Latent tendencies, recollections, or mental impressions stored in the causal body, responsible for reincarnation.

Yantra – Yantra is a mystic or symbolic image used for spiritual practice, traditionally used for worshipping deities or in tantric rituals.

Printed in Great Britain
by Amazon

12415081R00092